With
Love
and
Everlasting Gratitude

Paula
Maui 2019

# Masters of Belief

*of*

A Guide to Spiritual Liberation

## Felipe Zimmer

BALBOA.
PRESS

A DIVISION OF HAY HOUSE

Balboa Press books may be ordered through booksellers or by contacting:

Balboa Press
A Division of Hay House
1663 Liberty Drive
Bloomington, IN 47403
www.balboapress.com
1 (877) 407-4847

Because of the dynamic nature of the Internet, any web addresses or links contained in this book may have changed since publication and may no longer be valid. The views expressed in this work are solely those of the author and do not necessarily reflect the views of the publisher, and the publisher hereby disclaims any responsibility for them.

The author of this book does not dispense medical advice or prescribe the use of any technique as a form of treatment for physical, emotional, or medical problems without the advice of a physician, either directly or indirectly. The intent of the author is only to offer information of a general nature to help you in your quest for emotional and spiritual well-being. In the event you use any of the information in this book for yourself, which is your constitutional right, the author and the publisher assume no responsibility for your actions.

Any people depicted in stock imagery provided by Getty Images are models, and such images are being used for illustrative purposes only. Certain stock imagery © Getty Images.

Print information available on the last page.

ISBN: 978-1-9822-2110-2 (sc)
ISBN: 978-1-9822-2109-6 (hc)
ISBN: 978-1-9822-2137-9 (e)

Library of Congress Control Number: 2019901329

Balboa Press rev. date:  02/19/2019

# INTRODUCTION

We seldom read a book understanding and absorbing everything on the first reading. Incredibly, that which a person is currently not ready or open to receiving will not be understood, whatever the message. Oftentimes, that person will pick up the same book a while later and see it with entirely new eyes. At times, it will truly seem like a different book. It is, in fact, the same book; you are just different every time you pick it up. Some books can transform the lives of their readers; this is one of them, and it just might transform yours.

Let me tell you how this book came about. I was born into a family where almost no one talked about spirituality, God, self-awareness, or any type of religion for that matter. My family helped me with many things, but these subjects were like distant worlds to them, about which I did not hear comments. I had spontaneous spiritual experiences, which are not the same as religious experiences. At that time, I didn't intellectually comprehend what was happening nor did I discuss it with anyone. As I grew up and became more intellectually mature, I began to have a slightly better understanding of my earlier experiences. For many years, I closely guarded my perceptions and sensitivity, keeping them to myself. As the years went by, both became more intense. My favorite experiences were always in natural settings, where I could express myself freely and interact deeply. Now and then, I would turn to plants to discuss what I was feeling. You heard me right. When I was a child, I believed they were the ones who answered me. Most of my relationships with people were ordinary; they were nice, but nowhere near as sublime as they were with the elements of nature. Nowadays, I see such relationships entirely possible with both.

When I was seventeen, I had a sudden spiritual transformation. I was in Southern Brazil, seated on a rock atop a hill surrounded by natural vegetation and a broad view of the river and the horizon. Back then, I didn't know anything about meditation, but, for some unexplainable reason, I decided to close my eyes. I can't tell you exactly how long I remained that way, since time had vanished. I felt in harmony with life's very own heartbeat and inexplicably connected to everything — I was in *ecstasy*. At that moment, the "I" that I had believed myself to be, it was no more. That "I" vanished. When I opened my eyes, I felt as if I had awakened from a long sleep, as if I had come home. From that moment on, many things began to happen every day. Content emerged from my consciousness, leading to profound transformations with each new day. Another effect I began to feel was a slightly greater understanding of what lies behind illusory appearances and structures in both the human mind and society. At first, I had trouble handling so much information since I didn't have anyone with whom to share my experience. Intuitively, I started distancing myself from most people and letting go of my previous activities, entering an unusual period, a time of preparation for what was to come, although I still didn't know everything that was involved. It took me a few years to understand what had happened.

Interestingly, it wasn't long before people who made a difference in this process began appearing in my life. I will tell you about that.

That same year, I went camping on a remote beach on the Brazilian coast with a few friends. We camped underneath some pine trees at the edge of the beach, the ocean on one side, enormous sand dunes on the other, and forest-covered mountains in the background. After we set up camp and built our campfire, we spent most of the day in the water. At night, we'd settle down to gaze upward at the myriad stars above. Something happened during this trip. It was beyond anything I'd ever experienced or imagined. I'll try and tell you about it without leaving out any details.

One day, I had the sudden impulse to leave camp on my own

and set out for the immense sand dunes nearby. When I reached that wonderfully deserted place, I took off my clothes and started rolling around, having fun on the rolling hills of sand. An impressive looking bird flew overhead and dropped a feather. I understood it was a gift and gratefully accepted it. After a while, I spotted a man in the distance; he was walking the dunes alone. When I saw him, I got dressed again and sat atop one of the dunes. I just sat there observing the vastness of the place, just like the man on his sandy pilgrimage. It was a beautiful scene; he looked like a desert traveler. The man looked attentively at me from afar, then turned around and walked towards some bushes. I got the impression he was talking to something. He stood there for a while rubbing his beard, like someone having an inner realization. I watched him for a while then I got up to walk back to camp. I had taken a few steps on the dunes away from him when I turned around to look back. The man also turned around to look at me and started running slowly to reach me. We were at a certain distance from each other and I kept walking slowly. As he neared, he said, "My friend, wait a minute, I need to talk to you! Don't be afraid, I just want to talk to you."

I didn't quite understand, but I said, "Sure," and waited for him to speak. We stood facing each other and I was able to observe him. He was somewhere between the age of 40 and 50, with brown hair and a thick beard. He was shirtless and his body was strong, somewhat tall, and exuded a strength that seemed to come from an inner source. His eyes gleamed when he began to speak:

"I was walking the dunes when I heard a voice asking me to come talk to you. I know it probably sounds strange, but it happens. I have spent my entire life's journey in search of spirituality. I've frequented many religions for nearly 30 years. I've been a Spiritist, an Evangelical Christian, a Buddhist, and an Umbandista, among other spiritual philosophies. Nowadays, I don't belong to any specific religion — I just follow myself and God. The best thing that has happened in my life was when I found God in myself and in everything. The possibility of spiritual healing exists in everyone, but many people don't know it. I'm going to tell you about one of my experiences. Four years ago, a rattlesnake bit me not too far from here."

He raised his arm to show me the scar: two puncture marks left by the rattlesnake fangs. He went on:

"My entire arm was slowly being eaten away from inside. My body felt strange and paralysis was setting in. I spent four days in bed, unable to move — such was my pain. Then suddenly, without explanation, I knew beyond a shadow of a doubt that it wasn't my time. I felt this deeply. I expressed my profound gratitude for this feeling and prayed for a cure. On the fourth day, I felt a being full of light embracing me, placing his hands on my heart. Suddenly, my heart was aflame with a sacred fire. My arm started throbbing and the being said, 'I've come to heal you.' The throbbing intensified to the point that the venom spurted out of my arm. I was instantly healed. The strength in that light is infinite; though it dwells in every living being, few people remember it. A few have come to help all of us remember."

I eyed the man very attentively as he exuded an incredible energy. Inexplicably, I felt the sudden urge to embrace him. He kept on talking:

"I was on the dunes looking at you from afar when a voice from a Christ-like being of light asked me to tell you that you're here on Earth to help many people heal. You should remember that, though many people will come in and out your life, your true masters are yourself and God. You will play an extremely important role in the transformational process of the people back at your camp, of your family, and the countless lives you will meet along the way."

The man told me a few details about my relationship with those people and how it would all start happening. He described several points of my life in detail. With an intense glimmer in his eyes, he continued:

"Remember: trust yourself, have faith. Many people won't understand you, but don't let that deter you, you'll know what you're doing. Little by little, your awareness will expand. You will begin to feel God and his beings of light coming into your life, leading you to heal this and that person."

He pulled out a small book and gave it to me as a gift, an old book he had carried with him for many years. He told me to take it out every time I needed to remember. After I picked up the book and the feather, we hugged each other. He wished me the best along the way and to those close to me. We mentioned the possibility of seeing each other again. But to this day, our paths have not crossed again.

I went on with my life amidst intense experiences. Over the next few years, I had a succession of dreams that helped widen my perspective. I began to understand how to fit the puzzle pieces together and observe them. Around the age of 18, while communing with nature, a little of the material in this book came to me from somewhere. It felt like subtle blocks of information were slowly emerging. I had a feeling what they were about, but first, I needed to open them to see what they contained and then write down the information in a linear fashion. For an instant, I knew that I would write books, even though at that time I wasn't prepared to commit them to paper. However, I began recognizing some of the information.

Life has brought me several gifts, including meeting people who for years had experienced what I was experiencing in my life but had yet to understand because I didn't have anyone with whom to share them. Among them was a man who is a shaman, a medium who has worked in the area of health and healing for around thirty years. He isn't affiliated with any particular religious institution although he has known several. For some years, I lived in the same house and worked with this friend who helped me a good deal in the beginning, sharing multiple experiences. One day, when we were sitting together, as we often did, inspired, he said, in these words:

"The spiritual world is telling me you will write a book."

Years later, I was at home one day when I, out of nowhere, began to feel the emergence of those blocks of information once again. I felt incredibly well. This time, the information came more intensely, as if the entire book was being laid out around me. Then I saw a spiritual being in silhouette before me, saying:

"That which is to be written will be experienced in various ways. The contents of the book can first be experienced through you."

Around the age of 21, I spent several months in retreat, completely immersed in nature. During that time, isolated from technology, books or any human contact, I would go weeks without speaking or hearing a single word. An immense range of unknown aspects blossomed in me, putting me in touch with my own thoughts: attachments, fears, temptations and needs I wasn't sure whether they were mine or not, until then. In an inexplicable series of events, one by one those beliefs were naturally transformed, freeing those internal spaces. After these happenings, during my final month in retreat, the next few chapters simply began to emerge, completing half of this book.

After those experiences, I realized there was no need to isolate myself completely. I chose to lead my life among people, where I could share experiences. I returned to my city of origin and finished the rest of this book over the next three years. Furthermore, for approximately five years I chose to learn more about today's academic world by earning a bachelor's degree at a university. After these experiences, I moved to California to publish this book.

Along the way, I met a woman, a medium of rare psychic ability who has worked in the spiritual field for over forty years. Practically from start to finish, this dear friend has helped me more than anybody else in the development of this work, and we have shared countless experiences. Innumerable times, without her knowing anything, she used to tell me about what was happening in my life or what was to come. Other times, she received beautiful messages for both of us. We each simply knew what the other was thinking. Several times, without my ever having mentioned anything to her or anyone else about the book I had begun to write, she would describe it in detail. I would just listen and be thankful. One day, she said to me:

"You can only be writing these messages because on another level it's already finished – it already exists. It's as if it were alive. You just need to revise it, access it. What comes to you will be helpful for many people."

Every time, shortly after these occurrences, she would forget everything that happened. Her contribution to the development of the book and other events demonstrated that the work involved in writing it was beyond my normal mental capacity. In fact, in the face of everything that was shown to me, I see myself as being infinitely small, if not infinite. A tiny speck, as I do on nights when I contemplate the starry skies and they also contemplate me. The only word I can come up with to explain how this book came into being is that it was an inspiration. I didn't write it subconsciously, but at the same time, I was not in a state of mind I would consider normal. Some days, I would tell myself I was going to sit down to write, but then nothing would come to me. While at other times, I wasn't even thinking about it and out of nowhere a series of sensations and perceptions would emerge, leading me to write something yet unimagined. Each time, I saw and felt the presence of beings who were with me, like enlightened instructors. I listened to every piece of information they gave me and I would write about it. Oftentimes, we would talk about themes in the book until reaching a point of clear comprehension, which is something they always made sure I had. Several of these beings introduced themselves to me; they were part of an extensive group of beings who work to assist humanity. I say with deep gratitude that they were sources of inspiration in this book's creation. Over the course of the work, other intense forms of company arrived, assisting me in writing, such as the beings who presented themselves as children with boundless joy and compassion. All of these spiritual beings are just like us, except they're in a different state of consciousness. We are all spiritual individuals, although most of us have grown used to distancing ourselves from spirituality. These beings come to remind us of our essential nature. This might sound a little odd to you, or not, depending on your own experiences. However, what matters is not so much the participants, but whether what is written will effectively change your life. After all, not knowing who or what created Life itself does not change the fact that it is what it is, isn't it? The same goes for this book. This is our invitation, and if you take it to the end, you might find just that.

To make the most of its content, I suggest the reader to not get stuck in concepts, instead, sense what is beyond the words – the message of life being offered. The information contained in these pages does not have any semblance to the final and absolute truth since most likely no one could never achieve that in words. But it does contain something valuable for our times. I don't expect readers to believe, or disbelieve. What is written here, instead, can help you find your deepest beliefs and go beyond them. I have read this book several times, and with each new reading, it becomes a new book. May it be for you, reader, a new book for a new person; the new being one can be in each blessed moment.

# CHAPTER 1

Over the course of events, I found myself observing life intimately regarding what it provides everyone. As experiences arose, I began to discover something in myself I was not aware of, something that was already there as well as in the realms of the outside world. I began noticing with greater alacrity how life really is. Immersed in moments of doubt and questions, I opened myself beyond my mental meanderings. Afterward, these and other previously unimaginable questions were addressed, resulting in multiple experiences and ultimately, this book. Long ago, in my youth, as if in prayer, I wrote the following poem:

On one hand, death.
On the other, life:
An endless cycle of eternal music.
Where might our way out be?
Where will our wounds go?
A plunge into the vital principle
Casts us to infinity,
And death to us reveals
The secret of a danger.
Might it really exist?
Or is it only in someone's mind?
Something takes us somewhere,
Always making us observe.

*We can filter and absorb.*
*Might there be something to learn?*
*There seems to be an extravagant awareness,*
*Something akin to an exuberant connection*
*In which time and space*
*Are moving and motionless,*
*Set in the unity of divinity,*
*Giving rise to duality.*
*We behold a rainbow of sacred colors*
*From which, in a flight of sounds, come blended together.*
*Yes, it is a Universe of fluids*
*Created by a Great Mystery.*
*In the beginning I was everything;*
*In the end, I am one;*
*Or might I become none?*
*I may be in eternity,*
*In youth and old age,*
*As if united in a present moment,*
*Where all of my sentiment resides.*
*After all, truly, who am I?*

Felipe, have you found the answer to the last question?

*I believe I am revealing a bit more with each passing moment.*

We are, right now. We are all choosing who we are and what we want to reveal about ourselves. Our choices run through all levels of being, even not being, and are found in our actions. We are all like children in our essential purity, elders seeking to understand our own inner child through experience. Each one's experience, for what beauty is greater than what allows us to be? Value your experience, and it will value you.

*And so be it! Now, what can we share here?*

We will speak to people, directing our words toward everyone who is reading along with us. After all, books would not exist if not for the people reading them all over the world. Everything would remain stored away. This is just one of the thousands of ways to do it. We chose the written word as merely one of them, since there are many who are open to elucidation. May each person make the best use of it in their[1] own path, just as we do regarding the practical uses disclosed here. To this end, it is worth remembering the opportunity of reading these words gladly, regarding them as a gift received from someone else, asking the giver, "Is it for me?" If you accept the gift, you can choose what to make of it in your own life.

*How can we tell who is writing the book, you or me?*

This book is being written by you. However, it is also being written by us. In this situation, there is no defined difference between "you" and "us," there is no line setting us apart or isolating us. Therefore, we are writing it together. As we write together with and through you, we are one. What do you think of that?

*Magnificent! It certainly rings true with what is to come. In conclusion, I do not think who is writing the book matters as much as what is written in it.*

As we speak like many voices in one to you who are reading this book along with us, we will talk about subjects many people consider controversial until they become clarifying. We will bring a new vision for many people, one that, in different ways, is already emerging from various sources. We are going to talk about you in this book. We will speak about your relationships – personal, familial, romantic, social, professional, natural, and spiritual – just as we will talk about the Universe, our planet, and the circumstances of life where you live.

Let us speak about God. Yes, we will talk about God, since everyone lives hearing diverse points of view about it and many become confused when it comes to this subject. For thousands of years, society has been locked in a fight over the different images of God that have been

---

[1] The singular they (gender-neutral or epicene they) is purposely used throughout the book for the reasons of inclusion and readability.

painted for them. This confusion is reflected internally in nearly all of us. For this reason, we are going to talk about God, since this fight within us and among us is unnecessary. Moreover, since fighting is quite common among humans, the projection of their relationships in their representations is quite understandable. In light of this, the God presented to the vast majority supposedly owns the entire Universe and is in constant struggle with someone called the devil, his competitor, who would be in some remote corner of the earth, called hell, from where he would be trying to exercise some control over the planet. It is no coincidence that the two resemble humans fighting each other.

Now, you tell me, is that God? This is just an image of God given to you, nothing more. We can call it the God from the churches, or temples; incidentally, in these cases, those are more appropriate ways to start calling it, since there are several other visions of God. This is a certain historical view among many others. After all, even within churches and temples, the views about God differed throughout the centuries. Many stories told over the millennia are of symbolic and metaphorical origins so that people can understand the inner truths of the human experience. However, they have been broadly interpreted and distorted in a biased way. This has deeply influenced the history of society to this day and is still taught in the same way as general history in most of the world based on what has been passed down by a few prevailing cultures. The God of some churches was considered by many to be male, an old gentleman who sat in heaven and watched over everything, judging what he himself had created as good or bad. If you think that God is just one powerful man sitting in heaven, it might be a good idea to take a closer look around you. If we were to consider and integrate the history of other cultures and places around the world, we would see how biased people's visions tend to be.

There are other ways of interpreting God. Many cultures have separated life functions as they perceived them and created representations of different gods. In many cultures (actually, in all of them), there have been many names for God and his representations. Yahweh, Great Spirit, Allah, Tao, Brahma, Jehovah, Ra, Wakan Tanka, Viracocha, and Olodumare are just a few on the extensive list of names used in different cultures. It is not the name that matters, but the vision, sentiment, and experiences each person has toward a name and how they relate to it. Therefore, we are going to use the name God as well, since it is already well disseminated and deeply rooted in different ways in all cultures. Conceptions vary from person to person, but nearly everyone continues using the same word. So, let us use it, elucidating it, however, through a conception that aims to integrate all the others, even those of churches or atheists in a way that is inclusive of all parties.

Many people say God is a superior force. However, if there is a superior, then there must be an inferior. We tend to separate them. Other cultures perceived God as inferior and superior, exterior and interior, as being everything, where you and everybody else reside. God is not just something that is beyond you that you cannot fully reach, but also something that is around and through you. God is not just outside or inside, but also both at the same time. After all, not one of us came into a system outside the Universe.

There is not necessarily a need to be inside huge "boxes" like buildings, temples, and churches to be with God. A few persons in other cultures would see God as being beyond four walls, finding her in nature and its abundance, relationships, themselves, and others. Those called atheists are not those who do not believe in anything in life. Rather, among other things, they are the people who do not believe in the description of God given by churches, which they deny.

Your first experience of God arose with your parents or the first people who had a strong influence on you. When children come into the world, they look at their parents as if they are everything, the only things in life. Soon, they begin understanding that there is something to know as themselves, seeing their parents as their gods, as an extension of themselves. Even those who interact with the family during childhood, such as guests in the home, are seen as an extension of the parents or guardians. As temporary providers and facilitators, the parents demonstrate with each new situation what the world is like, validating life experiences, encouraging them to consider it painful or pleasant, each case having its own *particularities*. What a child receives and experiences during their first years will most likely be what they will regard as possible life experiences, along with their inherent tendencies.

The fact we call God Father or Mother is understandable, since they were the first experience of our perception of life, of knowledge of God. Similarly, representations of gods fighting among themselves are understandable, since many children have seen their parents fighting. The same goes for a God who judges and punishes, since that was the way some parents behaved. Some people believe that God cares more about certain groups than others, or more about humans than other beings, as if he had preferences, similar to the children's desire for their parents to love them more than their siblings.

There comes a time when you, as a child, notice the existence of something beyond your parent's world, different than what you had considered to be everything there was. Then you usually deny your initial experience of God, of your parents, opening up to perceive some of the other existing views. Although you deny what you learned from them, initially you carry it in your patterns, even while seeking new perspectives. When a child is raised in a harsh, rough environment, as they grow up, they may begin to deny it, probably unconsciously attracting something similar in their subsequent experiences; since it is what they know, is what gets their attention. In the same way, when they are raised in a nurturing and stimulating environment, as they deny their previous views, they will *probably* choose the more serene inclination to carry with them. When you were a child, regardless of the way you were raised, as you opened yourself to other horizons, you might have experienced reality shocks and may have considered them good or bad. It also depended on your preliminary understanding, and, mainly, your spiritual baggage.

Children carry a gift, which is their innocent way of being, closer to purity, awakening beauty in the gazes of people who see them. It is no accident that Life gives sparkle to the beings arriving in this world, a beauty and delicacy, natural to all species, impelling those close to the new arrivals to assume a protective posture. Speaking specifically and briefly about cases in which this occurs in harmony, oftentimes our first experiences are filled with care, attention and encouragement. As the child grows up, their parents and people around them gradually stop expressing incommensurable love for the child. They begin treating them more normally, since oftentimes they are still not in resonance with the expression of unconditional love. As the child continues to grow, the time arrives when they find themselves alone. They are not, in fact, alone but they might feel they are.

The person, who is now physically older, might feel incomplete, since they are no longer in their childhood-youth experience and still do not understand the other new experiences, and they begin to search for something. The denial and the need to search generated in this individual are natural at first, since people have different visions of the world, having begun their existences in different ways. To understand their initial experience, they may come to question it. As they question it, they will learn other views, thus getting reference points for new understandings.

Depending on how you were accepted in your childhood experiences, you will seek to duplicate it, perhaps in yourself. In other words, as the stimuli given by your parents when you were a child ceases, you are driven to make the stimulus that came from without into something that comes from within, transforming it into self-spurred action. It is called facing the world, but it really is your own self-expression. In today's conditions, rarely anyone experiences unconditional love, and it is possible to feel a sort of emptiness since the constant attention, trust and affection received as a child are no longer there. For this reason, the time comes when you choose how you will fill this modified space, which tends to occur during childhood, usually intensifying during the stage known as adolescence. Soon you ask yourself, what is this emptiness inside me? Needs arise. Many people seek to fill that void with romantic partners to make up for the unconscious needs from their first experience in the world; when that is the motivation, it is most difficult to achieve a harmonious relationship. Others will wonderfully transform that emptiness into an opportunity, considering the possibility of using the best experiences they had with their parents and guardians, turning that (along with the best tendencies they hold in their own being and other most pleasant visions yet to be known) into an internal movement of creation.

You create your own God experience. You are completely free to limit or expand it endlessly. Some choose to live it as something close to the initial experience demonstrated by their parents. Some end up choosing to live it as a negation of their former experience. Others do not get hung up on one model at the exclusion of another, but comprehensively include the best visions of the world, expanding their perception of Life.

There is no doubt about the existence of God. Not a trace. It might appear contradictory since this often has been the subject of discussions (and even wars) throughout history, but it is not what it appears to be. If you call him God, someone else will call her, in a different language, by a very different denomination. Also known as the Universe, Energy or Life. It is a matter of concepts. The question is not whether God exists or not, whether the Universe exists or not, but how it works. How does he interact with you? And how does each of us interact with her? The questions lie in *how* God exists, and the criticism is about the many different ideas of his existence. Clearly, there are doubts about the concept of a separate entity, but not about the existence of "all that is."

The doubt lies in knowing whether the idea of God each person has is only in their own mind, or whether it corresponds to something close to God's reality in the Universe. An indication of this is that no child is born with a well formed and enlightened idea about life, but little by little they acquire one and transform it during their journey. The same is true of the spirit, which modifies and comes closer to the experience and comprehension of the reality of God from time to time. The enigmas of these nuances reveal themselves in the patience and opportunities of time, in the immensity of the course of being, in the understanding to come from the spirit we always were, are, and will be. For this reason, we speak in depth about time throughout this book; it will be a new vision for many. The Universe interacts with us at every moment, in indescribable ways, but how we interact with it is in part related to the concept of God we have in our mind. In the course of the movement, everything has always been between you and God, between Life and your spirit.

How many of us sit among the trees, feeling the touch of the breeze while it rustles through the leaves and feel a connection? How many people looking at the greatness of the stars at night feel as sweet as moonlight? And although small, do they not also feel greatness when expressing love? How do many begin to discern synchronicity in the happenings of life? How many feel a universal meaning when they see their child being born? And how many feel a presence within them, and some kind of presence in all things?

God is another name for "all that is." God is a name created by humans, of course. "All that is" was not created by humans, since it has always existed and will always exist. Therefore, by saying that God does not exist, or you disagree with a view one has about everything that exists (for example, the God of churches) as if it were correct or final, or disagree that all that is exists. If you disagree that everything that is exists, you disagree that you are existence.

Let us call God the Universe, Life, Love, Energy, Cosmos, Truth, Spirit, Soul, Light, Being, or any other name that anyone would like to call him. Infinite are the angles from which all that is can be observed. We will use these and other terms throughout the book. If you do not feel comfortable with one or another of the names, use another one, especially because no name is needed to become one with Everything. Or you could use them all without any trouble at all. What we are proposing is not the name, but to get out of the box and see Life in everything, find ourselves everywhere, come to an understanding with nature, reconnect ourselves.

The completeness of this experience of connecting with Life does not belong to any institution, be it scientific or religious. It is our common right. In a fleeting resistance, many still encourage disconnection from our conscious nature. However, our spirituality is always within us, with or without religious institutions. How many wars, deaths and suffering have been and are caused by the way people deal with religions? It is high time to assume our natural state in the divine space of Life, all the time and everywhere, achieving the benefits of unity and love.

The way religions were structured generated a misfortune: the need for followers. To keep going, they find different ways of attracting the people who will support them. The impasse is that they need dependent people, many of whom are in the midst of an existential void and grab onto institutions, whatever they are. Nevertheless, we are not dependent, but free by nature. It is the reason we state that the best spirituality is that which is first from you and for you. That is spirituality, because you are a spiritual being having an earthly experience.

Many have associated the idea of spiritual experiences with religion.

However, one thing does not necessarily mean the other. People connected to religions, scientific institutions, or any other circumstance, can be spiritually involved or not, regardless of those connections. All you have to do is look into history. Both religion and science (as neither or both) are widely valid when we make them so. It is time for us to find the connection between all the institutional proposals, forming links between cultures and nations, in the much-awaited historical cure, edifier of a renewed world.

Religions could serve us better if they were structured so that, in spiritual sharing, people could meet in groups from time to time, since unity is the driving force of the Universe. We could develop different ceremonies without them being exclusive to this or that religion. You would not be Catholic, Evangelical, Hindu or Muslim, you would, above of all, be you. People would not be identified with a religious model or a profession, but with Life, taking advantage of the best that each of them could provide, whenever they wanted. A few religions have already adopted this position, or they are on their way to do it.

Let us take a closer a look. A scientist might call it the Universe, the Infinite or the Cosmos and is thrilled by the stars observed through their telescope and the atoms under the microscope. A religious person might call it God, Father, Mother or any other specific name and become enthralled when in intense prayer or participating in the beauty of certain rituals.

Religions may evolve and no longer depend on their followers, nor the followers rely on them. These would not be institutions hungry for devotees and what they have to offer, rather they would become opportunities. These religions would provide many means of spiritual expansion and communion, offering diverse ways of cultivating unity. They could function as gathering spaces for spiritual purposes, bringing diverse cultural riches that complement each other, stimulating knowledge and wisdom, making mutual sharing possible.

It would be like watching a movie. You would not watch the same movie of a single religion your entire life; you would watch any movie that might add content to your life experience. People could have cultural and spiritual riches provided by free transit in all religions, exponentially opening windows to new experiences. There would not be supreme representatives of these religions, as far as authority, just volunteers who study and practice the knowledge that the organization provides. It would be feasible for all people to acquire experiences and participate in as many religions as they like to in their lives, even simultaneously. One religion would not necessarily negate the other. Nobody would be considered to belong to just one religion. All religions would have principles of integration between them, interconnecting each other like a living network, differentiating themselves through their unique methods of celebrating the unity of people. Different methods, similar essences.

It is like planning a child's birthday party. You can always choose different decorations, themes and activities every year, but the goal of the party is still joy and celebration, isn't it? You can experiment with different religions, ceremonies, spiritual work and rituals, as with science and your everyday activities in general, but continue using each of these as a way of expressing and knowing your freedom and diversity, human essence, not becoming dependent on the same model all the time. The level of awareness and open mindedness among individuals can be incredibly more profuse, making sharing unlimited. Compared to other phases of history, more rigid in their organization, this is now occurring more and more. Why has this not happened widely? Because we are the ones who need to do it, in our lives, not God separately.

It is possible to do this right now, being and knowing ourselves and the different views of the world without limiting ourselves. You are the priest, a conduit of information. We are all sensitive in this way, we all have psychic ability. Let us first learn about it in ourselves and balance it. We are all energy mediators and channel most of we can perceive. Each being can know and harmonize themselves; by knowing ourselves we also know our neighbor. Always begin with yourself. By getting to know ourselves first and then the others, we will know how to connect with other individuals and in groups. Finally, we will know how to connect as a society.

Felipe, recite that other short poem you wrote some time ago.

*Which one are you talking about?*

The short, simple one, in which you talk about God.

*Okay, here it is:*

> *I decided to bathe myself in God,*
> *In marvelous waters;*
> *However, all the water that comes down,*
> *Will fall from me sooner or later,*
> *And this bathing in the water will end;*
> *But now, I shall bathe myself in air;*
> *Since God is everywhere.*

# CHAPTER 2

L et us begin with a simple parable that carries a valuable lesson. Two siblings lived in a small house in an inner-city neighborhood. Their names were Mary and Peter. Growing up, they both heard a great deal of talk about unconditional love; they listened to many stories from different people who shared their own beliefs. Some would say, "Unconditional love doesn't exist, it's a utopian concept." Others would say, "Love is the best part of human beings, but I've been unable to experience it unconditionally in my daily life." The two siblings listened to these stories in amazement, with a touch of curiosity, but were unable to understand. The siblings began to notice that those who declared that such level of love did not exist seemed to hold onto heartache and resentment, that they repressed their feelings in a strange way. Mary and Peter looked with admiration at those who saw this possibility of love as attainable; while seeking the state of love, these friends seem hopeful, yet still frustrated at their inability to take action.

After reflecting on the people they had met over the years, the siblings decided that the search for unconditional love was something worth endeavoring. They each made their own efforts on this new path, although they came up with similar results. Not unlike the hopeful friends they once met, the two siblings experienced moments of frustration, reflecting on all the ways they could love and perhaps be loved. The siblings were annoyed with themselves, indignant at their own feelings because they saw conditional love in themselves;

they oscillated between fears and attachments. Mary and Peter cared too much about other people's attitudes, who had a will of their own, making it difficult for the siblings to exercise their own will.

One day, Peter and Mary were standing in front of the house, talking about their questions, pondering over their inquiries and complaints. Suddenly, at the end of the street, they saw a man walking towards them. The siblings had met this man many years ago; he was someone they both considered good-hearted. Upon meeting him, they greeted each other and remarked on how long it had been since they had seen each other. Noticing that something seemed to be bothering the siblings, the old friend, in a gentle and understanding manner, asked what was troubling them. Mary and Peter felt comfortable with their old friend and briefly told him about their inner struggles, the difficulty in carrying out their search. Sensing the man's peace of mind, they asked his opinion about unconditional love, something they viewed as complex.

With a mixture of vigor and calmness in his speech, and after a moment of observant silence, the man told the following fable:

"This street's a little secluded, we all know buses don't run here, don't we?"

Even more confused by the apparent change of subject, the siblings exchanged glances and replied that no buses stopped there. Their friend continued:

"You see, unconditional love is like that bus, which runs every day on Main Street. Buses run one after the other, continuously, all day long."

"But what does that have to do with anything?" The two asked, interested.

"You've heard about this bus many times, but haven't been on it yet. You know the bus (love) is out there somewhere, carrying around a few blessed souls. You just don't remember the road that takes you there."

Upon seeing people pass each other on the sidewalk, he paused briefly. Then he resumed talking:

"Look. Between you and that bus (love), there's only one block away. But we see more people walking on the streets that can bias your perspective. As they pass by your house, some of them will stop briefly to tell you what they think that mode of transportation is, even though they haven't taken it yet. They'll tell you, "That bus doesn't exist. I've never seen it." Some will look at you, saying, "The destination is wrong. What's written across the front — it's a lie." Others will even nudge you insistently, speaking directly, "Don't go there.", when they do not say it between the lines."

"Confused, you're left not knowing how to go about it. Out in front of your house, you end up walking in circles and inquiring, speculating on the certainties or misconceptions to find the path. Based on others' opinion, you ask many questions and try to find the answers, even if you have not seen or taken the bus yet. At times, frustrated, you complain about your lack of success amid flashes of hope."

"There's one thing you haven't realized: to take the ride to unconditional love, you just need to make up your mind and walk towards it. Nothing else is needed, just your effective action. Although, if you believe in some of these other conjectures, this path can become more difficult once you're on it. The same goes for those who stop walking towards the bus, as they attempt to convince others to make the same choice, should they forget their purpose in practice. In these cases, it may be necessary to cleanse and let go of those old hurts and influences."

The two listeners exchanged glances, amazed with the depth of the story and how naturally it was being told. Then the man went a little deeper in his tale:

"Imagine what's behind the operation of buses that run continuously. There's a company responsible for structuring, maintaining and ensuring the safety of the passengers, according to traffic and local laws and regulations. You see, that company is equivalent to the spiritual realm, to Spirituality[2], fostering assistance, appropriate measures and the necessary structures for life, making the best possibilities available to everyone. Traffic and local laws and regulations are congruous with the laws of Life. Even though such rules exist, unlike what occurs in

---

[2] Throughout the book, whenever capitalized, the word "Spirituality" is used as a synonym for "at the spiritual dimension or at life beyond matter". When initialed by a lowercase letter, "spirituality" refers to the spiritual experience of one or more individuals.

traffic, Spirituality respects and accepts those who don't want to act in harmony with the laws of the Universe. It knows that these laws always function, whether you understand them or not, which is not the case with traffic laws."

"In the transit system, clandestine modes of transportation often appear, breaching local laws, changing schedules and even destinations. They lack proper safety measures, putting the lives of passengers at risk. Just like those who attempt to pass clandestine for lawful transportation, there are those who, in ignorance, confuse unconditional love with other forms of love, based on conditions and dependence, faltering in their choices and results."

"The best way, my friends, is to dedicate yourself honestly and purely to the truth within that leads you to walk in faith. There's no more precise ride than this, when it's awoken mainly by the state of the spirit, not of the mind. Acts of faith have never been exclusively religious. That's a myth, my friends, for it is a human ability. Faith gets you moving, knowing you'll get there. You already know the end results, even if the mind does not know."

"The main streets and avenues provide the necessary transport to the population, in the same way the veins and arteries supply blood to the entire body, like Love provides for everyone, flowing through the paths of the universe that constitutes and surrounds us."

The siblings breathed a little bit easier, feeling an atmosphere of simplicity. Therefore, Peter asked:

"And what happens when you get on the bus?"

Smiling at his friend's good question, the man amended his speech:

"Those who follow their path – regardless of the words others emit in an attempt to defame their mode of transportation and change their chosen route, or even better, those who simply care about the essential purpose of their own decision, will find it."

"As they get on the bus, blessed with unconditional love, they're carried through the streets of Life with a nice view. And as they see others lost in the streets, they'll wave from the window with joy and encouragement, inviting them to share in the good news. Knowing that their transportation is for everyone and that it's always running. Eventually they'll make the most of each stop or station, suggesting the way to the bus stop to any interested friends. Walk, but do it here and now, and you will find it."

The man said one last thing:

"Which form of transportation do you think is more open to all, local or universal? A bus or love as unconditional?"

# CHAPTER 3

I n our experiences, we will naturally come face-to-face with the forces that govern our Life, until these processes become clear to consciousness. We establish that they are indeed forces because they have an impact on our lives. All beings go through the same process, although these experiences may appear to have their distinctive characteristics. The differences are marked by the rhythm and form of each being's path. Insofar as we understand *Life processes*, we begin to support them, and they, in turn, support us (as they always have). We become open to the power and movement that follows this living intelligence, like water in a river's course, following the universal flow. This natural evolution occurs smoothly as we perceive that just because many around us apparently move against the flow, this does not mean we must follow. Some try to go against it and sometimes almost an entire society, but regardless of what they believe, everyone is in agreement with the processes of Life. Beings can spontaneously begin moving closer to the flow of life as they find it in themselves and everything else, facilitating the full manifestation of such processes in their lives.

There are several ways of looking at the universal system and its structures. Nevertheless, all structures are impermanent and subject to their conditions, or rather, they exist, but are not stationary. The structure of the universe is based precisely on this pretext, on an infinite and undefinable flow of energy, which is structured and destructed in the evolutionary processes of consciousness.

The Absolute is a field of infinite possibilities. The origin of the origin. It is simply where everything begins and continues, an "empty" field filled with all possible alternatives to a reality. Imagine this analogy, from the emptiness of an open sky, in the blank blue canvas of the vast atmosphere, little by little, faint clouds start to take to form, becoming denser and adopting a more solid form. Similarly, the entire universal process gradually came into being, in infinite proportions. Every single manifestation ever induced arose from a unity of possibilities. However, the question remains, why does anything exist?

Otherwise, if nothing had become matter or formed, everything there is would remain unmanifested in a vacuum without space, time or any other structure. To become conscious of itself, the universe unfolded itself infinitely. Thus God (Energy) went on expanding and expressing Itself as the only thing there was through what had yet to be a composition of forms. It is a natural process for Life to spread itself throughout the Universe, through the plurality of patterns and variables, forming galaxies, systems, planets, and geometries of all kinds, as in a simple flower, bringing the source into form.

Some researchers have been trying to find the smallest particle in existence — the primordial particle. However, where is the "largest" thing in the Universe? Its expansion is occurring infinitely in all directions. In the same way, it is infinitely expanding in every direction towards the "smallest," as if developing in an endless microscopy. In fact, there is no such thing as above or below, smaller or larger, except in relation to a point. Is our earth at the top or the bottom in outer space?

What happens is that a person's awareness is tied to a reference point, which means they do not tend to grasp these different relationships. If you quickly move through different points of view throughout the Universe, you would see its infinite unfolding and variables, which do not have specific directions, but it takes place in absolutely everything.

To make this easier to understand, let us look at what we call the seven processes of Life:

1- Change
2- Cause and Effect
3- Time

ption
ial
ividuality
ee Will

The first process to emerge was *change*. The Absolute source projected itself, causing a transformation. God began to experiment, the Being became existence in expression, generating the first contradiction of duality: formlessness and form. This beginning of manifestation generated a second process. The first change, being an action, became a cause. And, being a cause, brought about an effect. An action that naturally gave rise to a reaction. The second is the process of *cause and effect*. However, since everything started from change – always in effect and in constant motion, new causes were generated from these continuous alterations, modifying the pre-existing primary cycle of cause and effect.

In a closed system, cause and effect would be reproduced infinitely, since every effect would be cause for another equivalent consequence, and the phenomenon would therefore repeat itself, tending toward the same. A cause named "A1" would generate an effect named "A2." Having arisen from that origin, that consequence would become the cause of an equal effect. In other words, "A2" would become "A1" again to generate another "A2." A process of such proportions occurring infinitely and identically in a vicious circle. However, nothing happens in isolation. Touched by the process of change, which is continuous, new revelations are always created.

For this reason, change made it possible for "A2" to generate "A3," as well as giving rise to "B1" and a whole slew of variables, initiating a process of expansion of the Universe. Likewise, a consequence does not emerge linearly from a single specific cause, but rather, among so many interrelated variations, it is dynamically intercalated with multiple causes and effects, connecting everything involved. Therefore, cause and effect do not simply repeat themselves, they reinvent themselves.

The third process emerges: *time*. Such an event came into existence because of the differences in experience that was caused by cause and effect itself. In other words, the one who experience different causes and effects was continuously expressing Itself in the space continuum between successive creations and their consequences, establishing different temporal relations. The fourth process arose: *perception*. The one who was the experience itself was also the cause and effect itself, becoming aware of the living material of the experience since the manifestation of an action provoked a reaction and it perceived the impacts of its existence.

The fifth process arose: *denial*. Previously, that which observed sensed itself as "I am this." The change in awareness ended up bringing about the first denial: "I am no longer this (which turns into that one) since now I am that other one (which becomes this). The experiencer began to notice that, perhaps, it was not what it thought itself to be because it had changed, thus becoming something else. By experiencing that it was not something, it tested out denial, the apparent separation, perhaps the greatest of illusions (yet part of the Life process), ceasing to be all that existed in manifestation.

Therefore, the Absolute was able to self-express so that it could experience itself. Being everything, the sole source only had itself in the Whole. By unfolding into endless parts originating from a single one, it made it possible for each part to experience itself as a component of the Whole.

For this reason, the sixth process was born: that of the *individuals*. The entire manifested Universe is composed of infinite individualities, parts that see themselves as separate by the denial of awareness of the others, but which inevitably hold within themselves the connection with what they really are: one single thing. Every individuality in existence contains this memory, different from the memory a brain holds as a thought since everything from an atom or cell, a plant, a human being, to a system in a galaxy, all of them contain an essential memory.

The fact that this information is present in each infinitesimal part does not mean it is consciously recognized. What we now know as spiritual darkness is the result of the expansion of the Universe, a temporal consequence of unconsciousness brought on by the process of denial. Every living being, even humans, goes through the experience of not fully knowing who they are, each in their own way. When beings forget their true essence, what is known as darkness may appear to reign. However, in the depths of every darkness lives the light of immanence, which keeps everything connected. There is no absolute darkness.

Darkness, therefore, is part of the experience; in this case, all the individuals in the Universe, or rather, God, partially "forget" who they rightfully are, to fully remember through experience. For such grace to occur one of the greatest gifts was created, the seventh Life process: *free will*.

Human beings, since they are separate individuals, or better said, because they perceive themselves as being separate, become bearers of a "lesser" will. This lesser will gives them the freedom to choose from what rhythm and form within relativity they will choose aspects of who they are not, to finally return to who they truly are, through consciousness. Through the many multi-facets of the individual, these processes can occur simultaneously. There is a difference in rhythm and form between the experiences of each individual, guided by choice. This being a unified field, in essence, everyone experiences the same process.

The energetic force and natural intelligence that creates and is experienced by all is God in its pure will of divine expression. Divine will is the will of expression and evolution in Life. As it gave you free will, the divine will always imbue the lesser will, respecting your choices and helping you create your reality. Likewise, it aims towards consciousness expanding processes, while promotes in you a natural will to getting closer to God by your actions. In other words, God's will and your own are complementary, his will is your own will as well as your intention to get closer to the source of Life.

The seven Life processes (change, cause-and-effect, time, perception, denial, individuality and free will) do not necessarily take place in sequence, one after the other, but often coexist simultaneously. Freedom is the greatest gift of experience and is how the seven processes can be rediscovered. In fact, that is exactly why free choice was created, so that through it, beings could take the opposite path, at the rhythm and form they see fit. Through free will, individuals become free to carry out the final process:

## Unity.

When the *individual* uses their *freedom* through the process of *unity*, they find themselves beyond *denial*, remembering everything they are and everything no longer believed themselves to be, but which they never stopped being. Separation is no more, and they accept everything as part of their being. As they expand beyond the boundaries of what they believed themselves to be, the limits of *perception* are removed, making them conscious of who they are. Expanding their conscience through unity with God, they transcend the confines of *time* to intentionally become the *cause* of each and every experiment and its *effects*, being the *change* they want to see in Life.

In this way, the inverse process has taken place, and the being returns home, enthralled with Life wherever it is. This is what many call enlightenment.

It is possible to deconstruct several of the previously conceived ideas about enlightenment. Many people believe that someone enlightened is, somehow, "more" than they are, as if they were unreachable. But that is far from the truth. A master understands that being enlightened does not mean, under any circumstance, being more than anyone else. Nor does it mean being less than anyone else. In fact, it means becoming aware that we are one on every level; understanding that in essence, no one is more or less enlightened. Since if we are all one, there is no one but Us. There are only varying levels of remembrance and expression regarding the nature of what we are. A master is someone open to self-mastery, who turns a perceptive gaze towards who they are and determines their choices to manifest themselves in the broadest and fullest expression they can have of themselves as Life in the present moment.

In the same way, enlightenment is a choice as much as any other, although it may be realized at a more comprehensive level. Beings like Buddha and Jesus, among many others, did not enter such a state against their will, as if by accident; rather it was a natural result of deliberately surrendering to Life. The fact that it is a choice does not mean, however, that deciding that you want it makes such an experience to happen immediately. Although always available, even now, enlightenment is a process that arises according to the inner context of each one. It is not a process of doing, but of being, with each transformation of the present. The wise man is the one who delves into the experience of enlightenment. Choosing enlightenment is a claim common to all of Life's souls, in the excellence of free will, which in fact is nothing other than choosing to become deeply aware of oneself and expressing what is simplest in oneself, beyond any beliefs.

Choosing enlightenment is like choosing to become a parent. We know the simple act of choosing does not mean a child appears right away, at the blink of an eye. Every choice imbues a being with a series of situations they have to deal with, in real life, the experiences resulting from their choice, whether expected or not. Still, there are those who spontaneously enter the experience of enlightenment; even without knowing it was possible, they suddenly wake up, like a couple that becomes pregnant unexpectedly and has a baby. All the same, nothing is a coincidence in the manifestations of Life, and even those who wake up spontaneously (to the mind's eye) go through processes of transformation of consciousness, just as babies develop during pregnancy and continue to grow up in the years that follow. Expansion is the nature of Life. This being so, someone that becomes enlightened continue to expand their consciousness. However, what differentiates them from everyone else is their choice, how much they are aware of their own nature, in addition to the effects it begins to have on their experiences, especially on an inner level. Everyone chooses who they are and what they want to be every moment, consciously or unconsciously, along the continuum called darkness or light, since choice is the essential element of every being's freedom, accompanying them in the eternity of the present moment. Even those who believe to be immersed in the deepest darkness, as well as those who believe to be in the cradle of light, they are both immersed in the one and only energy there is.

There is no final, definitive stage of enlightenment since even the wisest of sages continue to redefine what is wisdom by entering new levels of experience. Enlightened beings are not identical to each other as if they were stereotyped patterns; they are individuals who are part of the plurality of Life, although, in essence, the nature of their choices makes them similar to each other, finding connecting links between such multiplicities. There are as many expressions of spiritual enlightenment as there are grains of sand on a beach.

However, the choice of enlightenment is not made at the level of thought but beyond, at the level of what is simply a determination of the spirit to experience the fullness of the Soul. Hence, because it emerges from what is, it is not linked to time; there is no need for hope or the belief that one day the moment of enlightenment will come. It is not a question of going "there," but of rediscovering what has always been here, even if gradually. Every being is already light since they always have been and always will be. However, a candle light surrounded by the darkening limits of a box is not unlike the process of enlightenment, when an individual begins to get rid of the barriers raised around themselves in the form of certain beliefs, concepts and tendencies, so that the light can express itself freely beyond thought. There is no need to light the flame since it always has been, is and will be lit. The Being's flame is eternal.

Enlightened beings know themselves and consequently begin to recognize themselves in the others, naturally facilitating self-recognition in others through their presence. With each person or being they encounter, they see what is most sublime, recalling the same potential in themselves, like someone who gazes at a child and recalls the innocence and purity within themselves. What in fact occurs is that the sage knows the fullest inner states already experienced, so instead of analyzing or judging, they *recognize* these states of greater amplitude in others, in such a way as to encourage, even if quietly, the best in everyone. When they come across an exuberantly beautiful person, for example, they recall inner states where they see beauty in everything, even though they are able to see what is physically apparent and part of what is hidden in the depths, they always turn their awareness to the state of their own consciousness.

Open to the wisdom that Life has given, the being immerses in unconditional love. However, not everyone remembers the path that leads to immerging oneself in such a state. To accomplish this, before anything else, you become immersed in yourself through humility. Many talk about love, but few understand that humility precedes it. The state of unconsciousness regularly leads individuals to point a finger of their own perception at others, projecting incomplete opinions. Humility is the bridge to love, leading individuals to direct their perception back onto themselves and to begin recognizing their own state of consciousness. If our surrender falls short of this, we may recognize our current condition, coming at least closer to enlightenment and love at the chosen level. Any approach will bring about intense transformations since Life respects every choice.

At this level of integration, it is understood that there is no injustice. From a much lesser and more specific view this may seem absurd to many, that view is also temporary, for the only thing that exists is the perfection of Energy. The process of cause and effect works for everyone. There are no punishments since there are no guilty parties; there are simply consequences, confirmations of every choice made, forming the living material of the experience. While on the surface many everyday events may seem pointless, not recognizing the reasons behind experiences does not mean they lack a basis. It might be helpful to understand that this process does not necessarily act in concordance with the time of physical existence (in the sense of creating an action and then experiencing the results). It acts according to the individual's ability to deal with their return spiritual experience, according to the appropriate moment for their conscience to evolve with that opportunity. There are universal processes of synchronicity far beyond the ability of the human mind. Resolved or not by the reveries of our mind, we are reawakened in the wonder that we call "God," who is all of us and everything that is and is not, in immeasurable states. The memory we spoke about, this connection, is in all of us. There is not a single being who is not essentially pure light, even if it is not fully manifested.

Although there may be no injustice since free will cannot be suppressed or removed, always complying with the experiences in which the being is involved. Still, someone might ask, how can we say there is no injustice when we look at the world, full of atrocities and tyranny? Naturally, through the existence of free will, individuals cultivate beliefs that create their experiences. At times, the belief is that the world is not fair, and, consequently, that is the reality we create in diverse extents. Every justice or injustice is the result of beliefs originating from free will, so that those who share this reality experience injustice when that is what they believe in, in their minds. Even standing before the cross, Jesus did not see himself as the victim of injustice when, as he as taking his last breath, said: "Father, forgive them, for they know not what they do." – King James Bible – Luke 23:34. Once again demonstrating the inexistence of judgments, crucified next to two criminals, once one of them, repentant, opened himself sincerely to the truth, Jesus told him that on that same day they would be together on the other side. – King James Bible – Luke 23:41-43. There is no injustice, nor tribunals, except in the minds of those who believe so, the only place from which this can arise.

Enlightened beings understand that the freedom of others means their own freedom, uniting their most dignified free choice with that of the other one, respecting their choices, without depreciating others' choices, internally and externally. From this perspective of expanded consciousness, each person's freedom is perhaps the most respected process of all.

Basically, there are two forms of dealing with free will: consciously or unconsciously. Unconscious choice occurs as follows. If you were to find yourself at a crossroads, with several different paths to choose from, without the slightest idea what any path is like, where they lead to, or even where you are, you would still choose to follow one, however, unconsciously. Although it might seem like you lacked a choice, you did: it is merely unconscious, until it no longer is. You might choose the one they told you to take, agreeing to it without understanding why. The more conscious your choice, the more aware you are of the essence involved in your act of choosing. This ability can vary at the various levels, according to the situation and timing of those involved.

The objective of Being is the expansion of consciousness. However, what is consciousness? Let us clarify the term and especially the notion the idea carries. The word consciousness is used in Spirituality as an essential source that observes, acts and flows naturally in accordance with the processes of the Universe, acting in the mind and mainly beyond intellectual knowledge, in the being as a whole, provoking infinite nuances of awareness. This is the meaning used in this book.

In this sense, as an essential element of Life, consciousness is a complete and ubiquitous field, a natural force of the Absolute that manifests gradually in every human being's experiences, guiding naturally to what is inherent in the Being. In accordance with everyone's moment, every act of awareness brings us closer to God. The emergence of a clear inner voice, insight, clarity of feelings or pure awareness may be manifestations of a consciousness flowing in you. Therefore, in this book, we are going to address the understanding of the gradations of consciousness in our lives.

As a spiritual being, every human has the inherent goal of awakening the expansion of consciousness in the now, in its unique way. The formless created the existential forms, which are manifest in apparent separation, so that the essence can become aware of itself through the forms, in a universal process of manifesting unity through plurality. Every moment of a being brings them temporarily closer or further from consciousness of the one source. Each part linked to all the others, and vice versa. Linked to the flow of the universal process, neither time nor space can impede the movement of the Absolute.

As spirits, we realize our potential by fully expressing the information of the miracle of Life, here and now, through the flow of consciousness, nourishing the whole: God. Beyond being just a word, God is another name given to the intelligence that keeps everything running, right now. This cannot be compared only to human intelligence; include universal intelligence, the intelligence of nature and of all beings. If everything that is known and unknown emerged from God as the Absolute, through real movement, you are also God but are not the only individual who is God. You are God in what unites us. We all are.

# CHAPTER 4

I f we ask someone about one of the circumstances that most affect
our lives, what will be the answer? Probably many would say: time.
The notion of time can be experienced from a variety of angles.
The intervals between seconds, minutes and hours follow a rhythm. It
is a way of telling time. If you were to choose longer or shorter intervals
for each second, minute or hour, you would be counting in an unusual
way. Other civilizations have had their own calendars that differed
from our society's prevailing one, called the Gregorian calendar. Those
calendars were based on a different reading of time. Different templates
based on a new tabulation method. Each way of dividing and reading
time works as a lens with a uniqueness that gives a new perception of
time. In this way, lenses act on the perceiver, changing their dynamic
in relation to what is perceived.

Clocks are a time differentiation factor, based on a system that
compares chosen intervals to create the notion of time. The deficiency
of the clock's famous "ticking" hands is clearly understood by someone
who travels by airplane from one country to another. From one airport
to another, there are cases where you can arrive at your final destination
even before your original departure time, or the day before.

No period considered as the past, present or future really fits in a
clock's system. What is the present, a second? But what if you split a
second into ten, a hundred, a thousand or millions of parts? Which one
is the present moment? You could continue dividing it infinitely until

you see that there is no defined time. May it be that what is deemed as the present is merely the human perception of a moment? And what about the perception of other forms of life, such as plants? Each form of experience perceives time through a referential, not an absolute method. Nothing truly separates one time from another, since time does not run at defined intervals set by the hands of a clock. Only your mind and body are led to believe that. Real time is the eternal present, which, in addition to containing the undefined here and now, contains all the times of eternity. We will call it *spiritual time* as well as *eternal present*, in the emergence of another understanding, through a renewed vision that deepens the opportunity to know ourselves.

Perception of time is something relative, a function shaped by several factors. In the experience of the individual, it depends on three things: *space, observer,* and *other observers.*

Time and *space,* as they are conceptualized, correlate with each other, since an expansion of distances creates an idea of separation. This would not occur if there were no extension between spaces, and everything was agglomerated, as if all matter were concentrated into a single object. The comparison between intervals of space is generated by the idea of separation (or rather, extension), thereby creating the notion of time. Consequently, the quantity of energy that makes up matter, as well as the way it is distributed in space, interferes in the perception of time. Scientists discovered this when they realized that time was not operating in the same way on other celestial bodies such as the moon, other planets, the sun, or different places in the Universe. And, when astronauts return to earth, they age at a different rate from those who remain on earth. Different temporal notions, unimaginable to the human intellect, are possible on other subtle levels.

The *observer's* point of view is central to the idea of time, since it is you, as a spectator, who perceives it. Space and time are interconnected even in the mind. If you are in an enclosed room and move to the top of a hill overlooking the horizon, your idea of time will change. The observer is in direct contact with space when moving through different environments, generally causing subtle changes in their perceptions. With the sense of "self" connected to eternity and free from limiting beliefs about time, the spiritually attuned find communion with each moment they experience. Someone in an enclosed room may feel (as if) in the Himalayas with the same intensity as someone physically on a Himalayan mountain can limit (determine) their perception of time, confining themselves to one room.

As far as the observer's relationship with other spectators, let us ascertain the relationship of the individual with the collective. As said, each civilization has had its way of reading time, which influences those who, from the moment of birth, come to perceive it through the lens used by those who describe it, thereby altering the observer's experiences and reactions. They absorb the model of lens that other observers demonstrated. The other observers are found in the social groups and relationships that the individual cultivates, influencing them from the moment they begin to share space. Thus, in the vicinity of certain people, you can perceive a change in your notion of time, since each individual perceives time differently, even if it is a subtle difference. Let us call it *social time*, marked by the way people have been conditioned to perceive temporal spaces, in accordance to their beliefs about the rhythm of society and durability of a physical existence.

In certain ancient civilizations, including several indigenous ones, there was a different notion of time; at times perceived as a circle or spiral rather than linear. In some tribes, despite the existence of complex alphabets, there were no words related to the past or the future; all of their words and phrases were related to the now. For some, each event took place in the moment and they communicated in such a way that they were present, creating no possibility of escape from the reality of the present moment. This gave them the power to transform any occasion, in many aspects.

Although you use social time as a practical way of going about your daily activities, while you express your being in movement, you can simply choose to interact as much as possible with spiritual time, feeling in its presence the benefits of the magnitude of the eternal. In this state, the essence of the content that is in your experience becomes increasingly available to your consciousness, to make the most of it.

Let us consider an example in the now. Observe yourself while you read the words filling this book. Are you merely glossing over them, associating them with concepts already known, quickly and almost automatically? Or if you are truly present, are you making the most of everything that adds to your experience, illuminating it?

Currently, many people in society choose to live in a state of constant complaining about not having enough time. There is no lack of time; everyone has it. We have all the time in the Universe, all the time now, which is the only one that exists. Lack of time is an illusion. What really changes things is how you perceive the only moment there is. That is the variable. The difference lies in what you do with your time, and especially, who you are and choose to be in that experience. The act of complaining about not having time is a way of preemptively disorganizing yourself since the complaint is a statement of limitation. Say that you have time, that you have the entire eternity as a present moment, and the ability to guide yourself through it in freedom. Let us make the most of this beautiful instrument Life has given us, time in which to move around.

As an instrument of Life, time is like an ocean carrying a boat. You are the boat; the time is the ocean. Nonetheless, the waters left behind and the waters ahead all flow together along with the waters of the same ocean, which is time, the present that allows you to navigate.

# CHAPTER 5

Temporal concepts are the fruit of comparing the incomparable. Thus, time is a mystery. Although time is not exactly as it is socially imagined, it does not mean that social time cannot be used. It can have its purpose. Metaphors are used to facilitate understanding about something considered real, through an allegory, a figurative context that sheds light on something that is true, aren't they? Likewise, you can use time to minister your actions. Just like a metaphor is a projection of ideas and images through a story to understand some of the truth, time is kind of a projection of the Universe (God), where a story, lived by living beings, takes place to demonstrate the greater truth. Exactly like the game of ideas and comparisons done here, time is a metaphor of Life on absolute truth. Remember: there is no point in believing that the metaphor is the absolute truth, it is only there as the possibility to understanding.

Time is a mechanism of the All to express Itself in movement. It is an ingenious device so the soul can find ways to express its perfection. In essence, evolution does not exist, the undefiled Essence is perfect as it is. What we call evolution is only the process of expression of each spirit, where we can manifest ourselves, both as we are and as we are not, through the vehicle of our bodies, so that we can complement each other through awareness of action.

What is the difference between soul and spirit? It depends, since they are both just concepts, which have had their definitions mixed up. To clarify things, let us use the word soul for one idea and spirit for another, because there are no specific terms that completely fit the following conceptions, and they even vary from language to language. Some might even switch their meanings, or treat them as synonyms. Therefore, it is important to understand that there are two different foundations, and not to get too attached to the words themselves. In this case, soul means the level where you are one with God, where there is no separation. There is no "they" and "I." The soul is unified and complete, present behind all times and forms, without having any form at all. It is absolutely perfect, without making itself known. Essentially, there is no such thing as your soul and my soul. We are one, so what could separate us? We separate only in our ideas the source that is common property to all, divine wellspring, field of operation for the spirit. When we say, "your soul," we are only referring to the idea of your connection to everything that is, which is true for everyone.

The spirit is the individual part that moves through time to express the soul. We can also call it "being." It has no defined form, but uses mechanisms like body, mind and feelings, creating the means to exist. The soul comprises the spirit and all its channels. Nevertheless, the spirit is not the soul, but the link to its manifestation. Similarly, bodies, thoughts and emotions are not the spirit, but transient and mutable parts of its expression. Perfection is in the essence of the soul, the evolution in the journey of the spirit toward the realization of its revelation, in each instant becoming closer to the fullness of God. The spirit's purpose is to approach the culmination of the soul, knowing itself through experience by way of its existential vehicles.

To clarify the relationship we are in, we will tell you a metaphor. Spiritual time is like a web. A Great Spider has woven the web of all time, a grid where everything happens. Made of infinite paths where all possibilities are contained. Absolutely everything considered possible or impossible is part of this fabric, including what is disregarded. The main point is that this Great Spider is the only thing there is. She is one with the web because when she weaves, each thread comes from her. The Great Spider can feel every part of her creation as a whole, for in this interaction, what happens to the web happens to her, given that it is all her creation, as Absolute.

The Great Spider wanted something, to experience each tiny part of her web, so that she could know the parts and the Whole. For this reason, she divided herself up into multiple little spiders (like the universe unfolded itself into infinite individuals), treading their paths. All these little spiders are actually aspects of the Great Spider. They experience the parts of their creation amidst the Whole. What the Great Spider did, in fact, was to prepare a perfect system in an interconnected grid so she could express herself.

Being everything that exists, as she created her web it unfolded into infinite possibilities. One of the little spiders is similar to what you know as yourself today, an individual. Since a system of endless routes exists, each one of them has to make a choice. That is how the system works. She has free will but has to make choices, setting the system into motion. The tiny spider sees that walking along one thread leads to another one. As the web branches out, each new path leads to a new destination. As the little spider travels, she expands and increases in size; a little bit of the thread stays with her and a little bit of her stays with the thread. Soon they begin to rediscover themselves as one. Each little spider is to the web as each human being is to the world and the Universe.

Through her choices, she maps out every detail of her path, setting the infinite web of Life into motion. Some choices (like fears, attachment, insecurity), will leave her temporarily stuck in her path on the web of life. This can create a mold, a rut in the web. This rut is a structure that was set up through repeated choices, creating a determined destiny. In certain cases, when these choices are repeated and inflexible, the result will be as well. That is the cause and effect dynamic. Similar to spiders that entangle other insects in a web cluster, the little spider coils itself in the so-called self-sabotage. When that occurs, part of the little spider's experience has already been traced, predetermined by her. When she reacts (acts the same way) to situations, she will automatically have the same type of result. The way she deals with these results is the opportunity for a new choice. The little spider can have the same experience, but now, observing it as it is with greater clarity, transformatively, at a level of great change and healing. This is what the blessed process of creation is about — replacing the reaction.

Certain choices can lead to multiples paths and connections, marked by their openness and flexibility. In these cases, destiny is not predetermined, and we can change the results at any time, using our conscious power of choice. Effectively, in any of these situations it is possible to change the results at any moment. It depends only on whether we are in conscious harmony with the spirit. The future is at most an inclination, which may or may not be modified. At every moment, the possibilities for the future are more or less laid out and changed —it all depends on our choices. What was previously an emerging possibility may no longer be one as new possibilities are always presenting themselves here and now. Among those, we determine. Nothing in the system of life is set in stone. When someone who can predict the future does this for you (or in cases in which it happens through yourself), what they are predicting are the propensities based on your previous choices, *conscious or not*. It is up to you to make the most of this opportunity, choosing whether you would like to continue building that path or whether you would prefer to change it. *Every foretold future can be altered.* The very act of looking at a foreseen future begins to build it or change it.

As immortal spirits, we carry our baggage of eternal life, and a considerable number of those past experiences interfere in our current lifetime without us even being aware of these occurrences. Incarnation is the existence of a spiritual being having an experience with a physical body. The act of disincarnating is the death of the physical body, as the continuation of consciousness, beyond the familiar social paradigm. There are consciousness interacting on different planes and levels, influencing each other.

What is established as the future is determined by each individual, both internally and in how they relate with the exterior world. Everything is a possible direction. Each act or emotion, each thought or intention is a new choice in the form of directed energy. All projected energy finds its path since everything is energy. Therefore, past, present and future interpolate into one; all belong to the present moment, the only time there is. In the eternity of the moment lies the extent of the

Great Spider's web. Everything else is the mechanism of perception and different points of view. Each little spider is like all the others, and to be means to be perceived; and so, consciousness is also experienced through the eyes of somebody else. The more we become ourselves, the closer we are to the core of our fellow creatures.

# CHAPTER 6

We can move our bodies anywhere, but in fact, we are only moving in the present moment. We are accustomed to thinking we are continually moving toward the future when the present moment is all there is. The idea of memory also creates the perception of time. Therefore, with an open and attentive mind to the present, there is no separate and faraway past and future, there is only observation and action here. We move ourselves in the now and while we cannot entirely leave it, we can be fully in it.

Each memory we have is some kind of illusion that does not correspond to the reality of past events. We acquire new concepts daily or reformulate existing ones through our thoughts. Each new concept is incorporated and added to all our recollections, changing them according to the content of those concepts and respective emotional states. Considering the influence environments have on all of us, how we view our reminiscences is easily changed according to our perception of the environment in which we are. Depending on with whom and where someone is, they will likely tell or remember the same story differently, from different points of view. As the years go by, memories are also remembered differently and take on other meanings. No recollection accurately describes an occurrence, but rather it depicts the meaning we reassign to our past experiences in the present time. Anyone can change the angles from which they view their recollections, changing them in their mind each moment. Nevertheless, it matters not whether they give them positive or negative meanings since they are still illusions. Therefore, observe how you move in the present time, whether you are merely ascribing new meaning to your past experiences or projecting your future ones, it is always done in the now.

We can say that this is a necessary illusion to the process since the mind uses our recollections, concepts and projections to coexist in the experience of the world. The idea of trying to forget something that happened is unnecessary because, unless a memory loss occurs, you will obviously remember your experiences, and that is not a problem. The difference lies in how we deal with those tools, how we use them. The fundamental question that is helpful in any process is never what was done in the past or what can be done in the future, but what we can do now, how we deal with those memories and projections right now; how we see them currently. We maintain that a clear way of seeing them is always available; is not only about changing our ideas about recollections – which are illusions— but also the level of consciousness. If you have been told that you cannot change your past, your experience holds a greater truth than this, once you stop considering recollections and new belief systems as belonging to the past or future, and conceive them as an integral part of your present.

Since no memory will ever be an exact match of what really happened, recollections are not a part of the past, but form a new reality in the present. *You choose how you want to perceive them at any moment.* This new understanding of time demonstrates that this moment is the only time there is, and that what is still classified as past and future, as if they were separate, is nothing more than different frames of reference, drawn anew in the here and now, in constant renewal. Whenever we separate time into conceptualized parts, we tend to distance ourselves from the ability to change situations as we would like to in the moment, because we dissipate such ability into constant illusions, held by thoughts of memories and projections that wander aimlessly in the idea of a past and a future. We may change the way we look at time if we come to see it not as something that was there, but as something always influencing the here and now, modifying its meaning. This is more than a new reform to the concept of time in physics, since it also includes a reform to the concept of time in psychology.

Looking to the past does not necessarily mean renouncing life in the present, it depends on how you do it. If you look at a recollection of yours or somebody else's using the treasure of love, you will recreate that experience in its present facet with beautiful dignity. As you look back on the supposed "hell" of an experience and you leave a bit of that affable treasure along, like bringing a piece of "heaven" where is needed, that past becomes a new present. There is no reason to look to the past or future except to bring this treasure or take from it. Difficulties only arise when we look to "other times" from this angle: to escape from the now.

All trauma is an established idea that lingers in the mind, consequently generating emotions that eventually affect the physical body. But if you change your perception, sensation and meaning of a recollection at this moment, healing ensues. You cannot change your past in the past, but you can change your consciousness about the past in the present, which is the same as transforming your past. By the same token, what is recognized as the future is the result of earlier choices; in this new consciousness, changing your choices here and now will instantly bring about a change in the results.

Evolution does not necessarily mean that you will have a mighty intellect or an impressive memory, although these mechanisms can be used. The process involves becoming whole with each moment lived, finding the simplicity of the present once again, when it becomes the integration of all times into one. When we become used to glimpsing time only according to our body and our mind, we will only see the past and the future they have created. The whole of eternity is in the infinite now, in the changeability of the present moment.

People often enter states, which if we look at them clearly are momentary bouts of insanity, although they are normalized. In these states, they assail each other with thoughts, words, emotions and, consequently, physically. Some concepts have been culturally reinforced by everything from advertising to everyday personal relationships, and when unconsciously accepted, generate changes in worldviews and in all relationships.

The redefinition of these mental spaces can be functional to the extent that there are memories, concepts, and projections of the mind that are keeping you from being who you really are. When the innermost of the mind becomes pure and transparent, far from the martyrdom of guilt and suffering over thoughts and emotions, the windows of the mind open to the flow of who you are and really want to be; opening the doors to the present where the possibilities to manifest are infinite.

It can be observed in personal relationships, when it becomes clear what makes sense to the human experience. Everything that used to be considered important, such as spending life operating through fear and in a constant state of offense or defense, no longer makes sense. Look at how people living in the same house, working in the same place, studying at the same institution, or nurturing a mutual romantic commitment often have difficulty relating to each other. They establish imaginary limits, behavioral patterns, distancing each other through concepts, assumptions and judgments that often make them intolerant in how they see and communicate with each other.

There are no limits to relationships between two or more people except those chosen, determined and accepted by us. Internally free of biased concepts, the essence of life goes beyond keeping our whirling thoughts in constant flight from the cause of unpleasant sensations. There is nothing comfortable about what people call the comfort zone, limited by clichés. These barriers are not unmovable, on the contrary, when they prevent the sublime expression of who you truly are, transforming them to know what is beyond those conceptual walls is to effectively know yourself.

You can appear to be going somewhere, but it is always within yourself, moving in the unique instant, connected to everything else. The outside world exists as a mirror to reflect yourself, since one does not exist without the other one. To change something in the express world (the mirror), you must always change it first inside yourself which is reflected in the "looking glass" of life. However, though it might appear that the Universe is something external to us, it is not. For we always have been and always will be within it; we are the Universe.

External change appears to be the spirit's main purpose; however, although this may sound effective, whatever it may be, it is no more than a secondary instrument for inner transformation. Inner flexibility to the intent of the spirit causes true inner modifications that are reflected in your external environment. Pondering the idea that the inner flora of the being is you, while metaphorically the external atmosphere is the mirror found all around you, we discern that changes to what occurs in the space around us originates from our inner space. If there were no real image reflected in the mirror's virtual image, it would be a vacuum without any reflection. Your experience change when you change. In other words, we create our reality. We change the atmosphere of this moment. We live in Energy, it is the law and each one of us generates it. Therefore, at the level that transcends appearances, there is no separation between the internal and external.

Perception is how we read our experience. The point of our consciousness manifests itself through focus or abstraction. The grace of God in your perception is between the states of abstraction and focusing, emerging somewhere in between, comprising the two states with the consciousness that flows through you.

When perception demands from us automatic behavior, driven only by repetition and programming, it profoundly limits the space through which a wide variety of expressions arise. The automatic state is only mental, a conceptual alignment performed through repetition. The automatic state is not spontaneous, since it is reproductive. Repetition can be a blessed tool when used by us, except when we allow ourselves to be used by it.

When we break an arm, for example, sometimes we need a cast so it can heal and return to normal. This happens with the mind as well. When we are born, many times the world still does not give us a proper welcome, with all the preparation and love possible; on the contrary, it offers numerous attitudes and words that are not beneficial to us and that tend to put a cast on our mind, programming it with a series of restrictive mental patterns. In the case of a broken arm, the cast is on for a very short time and then removed so the body can become strong again and return to normal. Otherwise, the arm would atrophy. But with the injured mind, this does not always occur and more often than not, the cast stays on for an extremely long time, believing it is protecting itself when in reality, it is restricting itself. Many people, when they reach adolescence or adulthood begin to seek to know themselves, gradually removing the mental cast formed in childhood. When this does not happen (healing the wounds, opening up to new ideas and consequently new choices), the mind begins to believe in the cast that restricts its ideas, atrophying the mind, just like an arm in a cast for too long. It is never too late to remove the cast from the mind, allowing yourself to come nearer to the wholeness of your being.

Many automated actions, or rather, programmed reactions, are based on insecurity, the fear of getting lost in the abundance of spontaneity. But, as with all fears, they tend to turn those who practice them into something nearer to what they fear, feeling insecure, or even inexpressive. Truly spontaneous actions instantly touch the spirit.

Different manifestations arise from silent observation, through attention. Hearing beyond what ears can hear, sight beyond what the eyes can see, contact beyond touch, taste beyond taste buds, smell beyond the sense of smell, and the silence is found. Something is happening at every moment; all we need to do is "listen." There is no need for boredom, there is no situation where there is "nothing to do," there is always abundance all around you and within you. Silence is like the colors of twilight, holding the night on one side and the day on the other. True inner silence is not found in the absence of sound, it comes with self-observation between yourself and the other, between here and there. Let us read the perceptions in our silence, for there is richness in any situation.

Receptive through attention, active in your intention. Where there is an honest and true intention, there is always a response from the Universe. Whether through words, synchronicity or any other means, intentions of this nature are always answered. Open the doors, open the windows, contemplation is when spirit sees through them. Contemplation is the state where you add intention to observation, add beauty to the picture, and add consciousness to the vast in the same measure that you receive it. Contemplate yourself and you will contemplate all things. By observing yourself you will finally begin to see which lenses you have used. To which concepts have they been set?

Expectations always limit experiences, for they develop when we mentally suppress life's abundant possibilities with a predefined model, trying to fit the experience into that model. Life is too perfectly abundant for us to limit ourselves to standard models of expectation. Attempting to do so is just like putting on blinders, like the ones they put on horses to keep them from having a full view of what is happening around them. Countless opportunities will present themselves that will remain unseen because of the blinders of expectation. We invite you to contemplate what is beyond the habitual mind.

If you want something, open yourself to the *original* possibility, the source that generates form, since this is the only way to maintain it. If what you want is a "better" place to live in, start by opening yourself to it through a feeling of prosperity. Do not focus beforehand on a specific house. For a better relationship, start by opening up to the feeling of love within yourself, do not focus on a specific type of person. If professional success is your goal, start by opening yourself to your creativity here and now, as well as your greater purpose towards the world. Do not focus only on mastering skills and earning diplomas, hoping for satisfactory results. When we are in a state of conscious energy, what comes next is natural.

We can limitlessly expand any experience, abandoning every kind of expectation based on preconceptions that will sooner or later lead to disappointment. Day after day, experience teaches us that systematic expectations become fuel for frustration. Expectation means an individual is fixed on the outcome of the form of experience, preoccupied with spelling out the details of how everything will be. Each person tends to experience something close to what they give space to in their minds, in other words, what they consider possible. Certain events will not happen merely because they are not considered a possibility. Considering what you want as a possibility – without elaborate expectations of how it should be— means making the most of the possibilities that existence always provides when you are open to its essence. Hand the details over to the Universe, the task of taking charge of the form of experience. We only have to prepare the ground through mental organization and by opening up our energy, remaining confident in our most genuine sentiments and the act of surrendering ourselves to action. When we act with our whole being, we are not worried about the results, for they are just a spontaneous and natural consequence.

With each new encounter in the intense crossing of paths and choices, an *energetic agreement of possibilities* takes place. Amid the mentalities of those present, there is an exchange of information, resulting in situations. With the beliefs of the first person and the imagination of the second, the volition of the third and the feelings of the fourth, the recollections of the fifth and the judgement of the sixth, the array of options at hand is compounded, made up by all of these circumstances, where each person is responsible for their own choices. An adjustment follows. These subtleties befall every time people share a reality. Without noticing, most of the time, energy is circulating between us at all levels creating our experiences even before we meet physically. A thought about someone immediately rushes to that person's field of experience, seeking out a compatible entrance. As soon as you desire to create an experience with someone, your energy will readily meet up with theirs to determine, from various angles, the possibilities of this exchange of experiences through an adjustment of all the energies involved in the situation. We are responsible for the doors of possibilities.

Human beings have the power of making changes right now, of stopping, at this very moment, anything that no longer serves us. If you *truly* want to be something: be it. If you *truly* want to do something: do it. Your mind may be filled with concepts that tell you otherwise, always repeating, "What about this or that obstacle..." depleting your energy. All that energy spent with your eyes set on limits is energy we forsake investing into something better. Let us set our sights beyond. First, know yourself and the truth you aspire to. Then take responsibility for the experience as a whole. Finally, open up to the possibilities that life can bring you. Experience is the living substance of spirit. Realization is in every present moment in which we find ourselves.

Your best intentions come true through faith and joy. The greatest guide to maintaining a joyful state is complete contentment. Laughter and a sense of humor serve as a frame for a beautiful work of art. We are here not to discover, but to rediscover ourselves, our intact and indestructible nature, to remember ourselves as essence—being and creating. You are a creator, the cause, with every intention, thought, word and action. You are creation, the effect, at every opportunity, experience, and sentiment. We connect with each other through all these aspects, in synchronicity, closer to or further from other creations related to our own. Imagine the following:

Just as if the wind inside a house "believed" that the surrounding walls and objects are its limits, many people still believe that their body parts, like their skin, are their limit. Even if the wind finds it difficult to flow freely in and out of such an environment, has always been, is and always will be the same air that hovers everywhere. Even in a closed room, changes in the air outside in terms of temperature or humidity will always bring about variations in the air inside the room. You can turn on a device like an air conditioner to change the room temperature and humidity, but as soon as you turn it off it will once again come close to matching the outside air characteristics, even if the room is closed. You can temporarily condition your mind, in the same way you condition the air. However, both will eventually go back to being close to their nature, to the relationship with the oneness. That is what eternity is for.

Regardless of the limits, *whether walls or bodies*, they do not separate what is supposed to be inside from what is outside; it only keeps them temporarily in different conditions. Still, there is meaning in it. It is more propitious for the air in the room to realize its boundaries and understand who it is while touching the walls, flowing around objects, or seeking gaps to move through. It would be more complicated for the air to understand who it is if it were free in an empty atmosphere, wandering great distances, promenading through immensity. The same thing transpires between you and your body. It is easier for you to understand who you are when you use your body, sensing certain structures, feeling it, caring for it and manifesting yourself in space and time. It would be more complicated for you to understand who you are if you exist only as a thought, wandering great distances, promenading through immensity. That is the gift of experience.

If the wind were to discover itself in a closed environment, by coming into contact with supposed limits, it could observe who it actually is by contrast. Upon returning to the freedom of the all-encompassing air in the sky, it carries with it the consciousness of what it learned about itself. In the same way, every human being who experiences being in a body, through the discovery of its supposed limits is able to remember who they are. As they return to their source (from where they never left), they become more deeply aware of who they are. As if the air, upon returning to its beautiful nature, gradually understands itself through its experiences – the same happens with us.

That is the wonder of reincarnation, pre-existence and post-existence. Many times, the air will find itself experiencing environments that restrict its freedom, like a little game in different rooms or halls. Each time it moves from one place to another, it carries with it a little more awareness along of both, its totality and the limitations that highlight that totality. You may often find yourself experiencing a body that apparently limits your freedom, through different existences. However, every time your perception moves back and forth from one level to another, you can bring along a little more consciousness of your experiential baggage, both of the totality of your soul and the limitations you came to know that emphasize that totality. The expansion of consciousness is what we carry into eternity.

Just as if the wind knew that it is free and not afraid of the limits it faces, dancing in the air and environments, individuals, rather than using their bodies and becoming claustrophobic with their apparent limits, can understand how to love in all places and flow in all situations. Only playing at creating and dancing between existences. Reincarnation is not about the improvement of the soul or its evolution, but rather of the human spirit that incarnates and journeys to express the totality of its soul in action. Reincarnation is an opportunity for the expansion of consciousness, embracing the knowledge of who we really are through what we are temporarily. Since all of us are life and Life is eternal, it is not lost or destroyed, only transformed.

Essentially, creation does not come from nothing because all possibilities already exist. Creation means effecting transformation based on everything there is; it means choosing to express one portion of the All at a time, in the same way the wind is continuously transformed in its spiraling movement. There is nothing new for the soul, nothing to develop, since everything has always been, is and will be there for it. For each spirit, there are only the infinite possibilities of how to remember and express this glorious presence, whenever it desires and as many times as it wishes.

# CHAPTER 7

I n various cultures and civilizations, there have been human beings aware of their lives and interaction with the Universe. Societies around the world have made similar observations, each in their own way, collectively and individually. These civilizations became aware of the principle of duality in the workings of life.

Cultures have given different names to these principles. In the Far East, the Chinese called it *yin* and *yang*, respectively being passive and active, feminine and masculine, above and below, left and right, night and day, visible and invisible, and so forth. In India, many maintained that duality is an illusion, which they named *Maya*. We might add that this illusion is not the same as a mirage that one would experience in the desert when seeing an oasis that is not really there. The meaning of the word "illusion" does not invalidate what is perceived as such, however limited, but to point out that there is something beyond that duality.

Imagine one of our ancient ancestors standing on the beach, without any geographic knowledge. They behold the sea on one side and land on the other. The illusory state would tell them that the land they see on one side and the water they see on the other, separated by the stretch of beach on which they stand, is all that exists. To them, the sea only reaches as far as their eyes can see and the same goes for the land. What they don't know is that beyond their sight, land and ocean extend and interlace to form our immense and fully connected planet Earth. In their experience, the illusion is the limits established by the mind, making them seem insurmountable. The illusion of duality consists of seeing only appearances, whereas unity connects all that transcends this condition.

The earth supports and nestles the sea. Water evaporates and is carried away in clouds by the wind, then falls as rain on the fields, plains, and plateaus, it mixes with the soil and fills the earth with the lives that sprout from this union. Each fruit, for instance, does not come from the branches of a tree alone. Take an orange, a simple fruit of vibrant color. Did its tree, the great orange tree, grow from a tiny seed? Did it come from the seed alone? The plant, a magnificent living being, coupled itself with the earth and the water from distant sources, loading itself with nutrients and vitality, generating the orange tree and the orange as a result of this union.

The perceptions of all peoples can complement one another since both duality and what lies beyond, are manifestations of the Absolute. God is in unity and also in duality, after all, being the Absolute everything that exists and even that which does not exist, how could anything be placed outside the All? Here is where we begin to observe these foundations interact in several ways.

*Health* and *disease*, as well as *life* and *death*, are aspects of this dichotomy. To manifest, one cannot exist without the other; however, they are the same under different configurations. For them to happen, they act as complementary opposites, but fundamentally, there is only one. Illness and death deteriorate a body, which goes on to furnish life to animals or plants. The body always returns to Earth as life for the sphere. There is only Life and its movement so that when you die and disincarnate, your consciousness continues to live. Essentially, Life is all there is and it uses death to manifest itself.

People live the experience of separation; nonetheless, they have never truly been separate. Throughout the Universe, countless spirits are experiencing themselves as individuals, but what set the boundaries between one and the other? Fundamentally, we are all the Great Soul manifesting itself, as in the earlier example of unity between the oceans and the Earth. The multiple individualities are the way the Great Spirit expresses itself.

*Light* and *darkness* are aspects of duality. One does not exist without the other, despite this, there is but one. After all, darkness is simply the absence of light so that everything is light just like the stars that paint the sky. Equally, *cold* is merely the absence of *heat*. Then consider *absence* and *presence*; where would the absence be if the Universe is found in everything and everyone? In some ways, you are present in everything and everyone. We are interconnected; is there anything that is not connected to everything else?

In some cultures, many individuals have observed only the process of duality, while others only unity. However, true union resides in the unity of the perception of both the duality and unity. Saying that true union means perceiving both sounds like a dichotomy, does it not? In fact, unity is all there is, and it only makes use of the polarities (and all the variables) to manifest itself.

The human mind is unable to understand the Universe in a real, infinite, and complete way for it is not absolute, only an instrument. Yes, some things are indeed part of a great mystery beyond our rational comprehension. Does that sound too *complicated*? Would it be better if we told you everything is *simple*? Everything simply works as it is regardless of your thoughts. It may seem complicated when words fail because they are only tools and not life's complete works.

We could spend a long time playing on the seesaw of duality, but we will instead consider a few more cases that may be useful to the human context. Real balance is not found in the neutrality between the poles, but in unifying the two. Unity is almost like a third condition that encompasses the two previous ones.

Imagine a scale with life on one side and death on the other. When life begins to lose its vitality, death starts gaining weight on its side of the scale, until it outweighs life. However, the weights are only distributed on the scale not anywhere else because this system is all that exists. As soon as death prevails, the scale begins redistributing weights again and life reemerges, playing with the weights, balancing and unbalancing. Finally, we realize that Life is the only element that exists, redistributing itself. Even more, we realize that the scale is Life itself, setting the entire game in motion. The scale is Equilibrium and only uses *disequilibrium/equilibrium* to always keep the game even.

You can observe the same thing with emotions. Love and fear are aspects of duality when linked to the mental/emotional mechanism. Emotions like anger, attachment, insecurity, affliction, pride, and all the others conceptualized as negative are the parts that constitute fear. They originate from fear. For its part, fear does not exist on its own without love.

Emotions like joy, forgiveness, kindness, tranquility, gratitude, and all the others conceptualized as positive are the parts that comprise love. They originate from love. In its dual aspect, love does not exist without fear. You know tranquility because you have known nervousness and insecurity. Forgiveness, because you have known judgment and anger. Kindness, because you have known the pain of pride. Gratitude, because one day you knew affliction. Joy and freedom, because you have known confinement and attachment.

When restricted to conditions of a mental/emotional process, love and fear are also components of the two sides of the scale, so that one is always returning to the other, as if redistributing the weights. If you experienced fear and attachment before, and are now experiencing love and freedom, you might just harbor the fear of experiencing suffering in its different forms again. Who among us has never feared "losing" a loved one? This demonstrates the existence of this emotion, even if camouflaged. By the same token, if you are experiencing fear or any of its variations, there is always hope, active or not, of once again experiencing love and freedom. All of these forces are related. We go through this when we enter this cycle, experiencing through various incarnations and existences. Have you noticed that fear and love always walk hand in hand under these conditions? For some, this fact may be cause for sadness, but it does not need to be.

At the core, we see that Love is all there is. Not exactly the Love of cyclical polarity, but the kind that integrates, as the entire scale. One of them is conditional love, related to fear as one of the sides of this duality. Finally, there is absolute Love that integrates all the feelings into the most comprehensive of all: the Love of Life. It allows us to freely live through any emotions we recognize and learn through experience. The Universe makes this possible for everyone by giving us free will. Can you see how God is Love? There is more to come.

Unconditional love is the manifestation of the Universe's absolute

Love through human beings. When we go beyond the common mental structures with which human beings tend to identify, we see that all that remains in us derives from Love. Separatist views are only in the mind, and as it transcends the limits of its patterns, all that is left are natural joy, unity, a fluent life, as well as infinite variations of absolute Love. However, we are free to learn about all the emotions and feelings as much as we want for in the Universe, there is time for everything. There is time here and there, time that is not happening and time that is happening now. We tell you that, essentially, all possibilities are always vibrating, all times influencing the now, and vice versa. It is only the game of the scale.

From this angle, you can say that the Universe is usually perceived from three states. The first is the illusion of separation. Everything seems divided and fragmented. In this state, there are individual bodies, faraway lands, and untouchable and unseen planets and stars. It is where the belief that you are you and your neighbor is a separate being dwells. An effect of perception and appearance created by this notion, so that, by contrast, you can come to understand the essence and unity of all things.

The second is the Connected Unity. This is the state closest to the reality of the Universe, where everything is related, communicating with everything else in different ways. Everything is one, but operates like a web, which, when touched, reverberates an effect throughout its entire extension. Every action is a potential touch to the web, affecting everything and everyone through the connection.

A third state encompasses the two previous ones. It is the legitimate state of the Universe. Absolute Unity. Where everything is one, without forms or divisions—like a background that sustains all energy. It is our original state as souls, the original state of God from whom we never distanced ourselves, although we may believe we have. We can talk *about* Absolute Unity, but there are no words that truly contain its meaning. We are immersed at every moment in this ocean, yet, due to our condition as individuals connected to some type of form, there is no mental or emotional perceptual structure that captures the totality in such conditions. We are able to partially feel this immeasurable force and magnitude with no defined limits, in the spirit's own presence. As you enter the Connected Unity and perceive the connection even in the illusion of separation, you will experience the closest thing that every moment can give you of the manifestation of the Absolute Unity through itself and everything. Connecting oneself to the Absolute Unity means going beyond any sense of a "separate I" and aligning with the flow of Life and Love.

Throughout history, some of the beings who have demonstrated countless of these possibilities have been called masters, enlightened ones, sages, saints, evolved ones, etc. While they earned many names, the names are unimportant. They are only concepts. Beings like Jesus Christ, Buddha, Krishna, Lao Tse, Mother Teresa and many others are known (or not) by their legacy of expanding spiritual horizons.

To the extent individuals find unity, they begin to resemble the metaphor of the scale. A master consciously becomes Life itself, for even if their body dies, they are always conscious of their living. As spirit, they experience the closeness to the soul's totality in its instant. They become Love itself, free from repetitive cycles, open to the embrace of the Universe. The Being sees itself as spiritual time, integrating everything that has been, is and is not in the eternal present.

A master sees light in everything. This does not mean they no longer perceive darkness, or deny it. They just do not see it in that way anymore. Now, they simply see every shadow as the absence of light, a space considered necessary but of passing importance towards the comprehension of the soul's brilliance.

All human beings experience their own cycles until they eventually integrate them, inevitably becoming masters of themselves. Enlightenment is not something to seek out as if it were a title to be won in the future, but the choice to realize the light of being in the consciousness of your own presence. Happy is the one who aligns themselves with natural consciousness, available to all the living presence, revealing itself to perception inch by inch.

To expand consciousness means subtilizing experiences over the course of time. The subtler they become, the greater the reach and depth of your assimilation. On an expansion scale, what you once believed to be subtle now becomes visible, while what you had not noticed previously becomes subtle, successively opening the windows of perception. This is why consciousness is dazzling to us and fills us with joy; it removes the blindfold that "keeps our eyes from seeing," so that we can fully live the extent of what Life offers. Soon, the cycle becomes subtler until it is transcended, undoing the unnecessary mental/emotional forms. The energy the individual used to spend maintaining those unconscious structures returns to their being, which once again manifests itself in consonance with the natural flow.

God remembers himself constantly through living systems, each one of us revitalizing the hidden essence. In the face of freedom, the capability of the Universe is infinite. Even though human beings forget who they are and remember, in fact, remembering is the only thing there is. We are always surrounded by Love, we always have been. We are immersed in Love, just like a planet is immersed in outer space. We all observe and are observed. Is there a greater miracle than the existence of observation? Every being is both a center for witnessing Life and a participant of eternity, and therefore, one only, interconnected in infinite unfolding. Can you understand now, even if briefly, how perfect is the Universe?

# CHAPTER 8

The importance attached to things is personal, frequently originating from a collective array. Not everything is intrinsically important. As the name implies, the root of the word "import"[3] *is the action of bringing something to oneself.* Just like professionals who process transactions in the economic sphere of society, importing products and materials from other locations to where they are needed, we do the same with the things we find important.

Everything we deem important we bring into us, in a constant exchange of energy. It is like a trade, we offer a little of our energy and whatever it is begins to interact with us. On the import market, transactions involving finances or products are carried out, such as when a country brings something from distant lands. Between human beings, these are affective, mental and physical exchanges, among others. Essentially, these are all energy exchanges. After all, money is only a neutral energy. Good or bad, important or not, it is a matter of the direction given by each person.

The act of attaching importance is relative, personal, and always changeable — we can care about anything. Things simply are; they do not lend importance to themselves. We are the ones who attribute more or less value to events, because caring about something is our

---

[3] In fact, the Latin word *importare* means to bring in, and is composed by *im* (in) and *portare*, which comes from *portus* (passage, port).

choice. Exchanges happen – we are all interconnected after all, and at some level we exchange something with everything and everyone. Just remember that whenever you "import" something, something in you is exported.

As you walk among the trees in a place of natural beauty, each side gives and receives a little in an energetic relationship. If you enjoy the interaction, the exchange can be more intense. It is no accident that some people feel at ease among plants and others not so much, since this is also a matter of connection.

If you attach importance to crime and violence, you associate yourself with this energy in the same way. It is a two-way street. You feed them while they feed fear and violence in your life. Through exchange, we become aware that any form of attention is an act of power. *The way we pay attention to something demonstrates how we feed it.* It is all part of our choices, but, are they good or bad? It depends on you. What do you choose for yourself? The time will arrive when we understand there is something more than an energetic exchange in all relationships. There is sharing, since exchange implies that each side gives and takes something, the act of sharing is a joint act, in which both sides share something, regardless of how it may occur.

When we receive news of violence, we begin to disseminate it into the world the moment we become emotionally engaged through fear, anger, revenge, or other emotions that revolve around such events. Whenever someone gives importance to something in order to identify with the situation through these kinds of emotions, thoughts, or words, they support the propagation of this situation. Violence is fed not only by those who practice it directly but also, on other levels, by those who cultivate those emotions because regardless of where they are physically, they are connected. Remaining in a state of fear, thinking "How horrifying" and dispersing such news, will not end the violence, it will only continue to spread.

It is not to say that we have to isolate ourselves, ignorant of the crime and current violence exposed to the world. If your intention is to stop creating this type of reality, one option is to choose not to feed it through attention and identification. The fact that we keep giving energy to these circumstances through the fear, rage, and violence they generate in us, does not mean we are protected from them. For some, the distribution of violence is a feast, as much as those rare messages beneficial to peaceful living are a feast to others. This statement can be confirmed by watching local or international media for a single day. Take the theme of "violence," for example, as you observe and become involved with this energy, ask yourself: *what is behind my attention and involvement?* Fear or love? If it is fear, the situation will tend to stay at the same level. If it is love, forces arise to bring healing and harmonization to the circumstances.

If you dislike violence, *do not go against it,* but rather, align yourself with peace. Simply be aware of the existence of violence and commune with peace. This is one of the principles of transformation, individually and collectively, since everything one resists, re-exists. Whatever we condemn is intensified. That is the nature of attention, something we can verify by watching an ordinary child who repeatedly insists on doing whatever the parents or guardians forbid, showing exactly how the mind works.

In Spirituality, all choices are simply observed since what determines them is a belief in the need to live certain experiences, where the spirit seeks to complement itself through multiple existences. Everything human beings consider evil is viewed solely as temporary choices, in the sense that people who proceed in this way still believe themselves ignorant to the workings of their being and the Universe. However, such wisdom is innate to the soul. Understanding and consciousness will come to all in the midst of eternity. Consequently, we do not judge any kind of choice. How could we, if one does not recognize the elements of the game of Life? Would you judge a newborn for not knowing how to talk? We understand that soon that little person may know as much or more than us. The time for conversation will come. We only see possibilities for help and interaction, if the situation moves away from these purposes, we observe with the proper respect and parsimony.

When we choose to live in fairness, one of the best ways is to follow a simple honest path. When you see someone on a path leading them away from it, with signs of apparent injustice, judging, criticizing or even focusing on them to force change against their will is a waste of energy. When you are on the path of fairness, *diverting* your attention and energy to focus on someone else's path and concerning yourself with their attitudes instead of minding yours, can waste magnificent opportunities on your own journey. The point is: leaving your best states behind to explore others' inharmonious states makes this practice pernicious. Those who go against what is classified as evil run the risk of becoming the same, but those who consciously face darkness, and do not fight or resist, only bring light to it. Act in favor of justice, and you will naturally weaken the remnants of the unjust. Being an *example* on the path of fairness is the best form of real change, reflecting upon those open to such greatness. Start with yourself, and it will spontaneously extend to those who are receptive.

Do not try to avoid what does not suit you, for whatever you are trying to avoid remains in your focus, therefore, you are attracting it to you. You can, if you want to, create consciousness and disseminate your best vision of the world. You can stimulate the beauty of life, seeing it in everything: freedom by being truly free, peace by being at peace, supporting consciousness when faced with something that no longer serves you, while opening and expanding it to the simplest and most gratifying aspects of everything.

If you notice something in your life that is no longer of use to you, start doing whatever you believe will be useful, thereby instantly transforming yourself into a better being. If war is part of your past, adopt peace in the present. If fear has predominated, redeem yourself with love. If something has displeased you, within or without, do not play the role of being "against it" since this will only stimulate it, rather, determine a new choice that pleases you. If you truly want a better world, *do not fight*, since every fight inevitably results in winners and losers. Although, from an even broader point of view, we all lose whenever there is fight. Effectively work on your inner conflicts, contributing to harmony, truth, and love. By being a bearer of light and equanimity of consciousness, undoubtedly, your/my/our world will finally be at peace.

If anything were to be considered inherently important, it would be the experience of God, which flows naturally. God is and permeates everything, in natural synchronicity with all occurrences. Nevertheless, since Life gives all beings free will, how could we possibly judge how each person attaches importance to things, even punishing them if they do not go with the most important choices? This would obviously contradict free will. Ultimately, every being and their consciousness determine what to lend importance to, at the right moment, changing during their experiences from causes to consequences, according to their choices. You have that power and responsibility. We all do.

The present is where the act of caring occurs, so we can consider it preciously inherent. Accordingly, everything we can call God, containing essential and eternal characteristics like Life, Energy, Presence, Absolute Love, Being, Soul, can be inherently important. What do we mean by this? Regardless of your choice or attention, these attributes of the Universe have always been, are and always will be in everything. They flow through you, behind the scenes, sooner or later, as conscious participants in the play. The rest is ephemeral. Still, whether we lend relevance to any of these singularities in any given situation, so they become conscious, is up to us. Electing something as relevant requires feeding it with our energy.

On the other hand, a state of indifference is common in people who care, but believe they cannot bear living with whatever it is they cared about, as they try to deny and resist what happened. Many people become indifferent to the human instability around them, but not because they do not care. On the contrary, they care deeply and do not know what to do. They believe themselves powerless before the facts and adapt. Nevertheless, it is possible to know, by consciously and calmly choosing the best ways of navigating a moment without identifying with the extremes of indifference or fleeting importance, but instead connecting to the presence of what is *inherently important*. While our choices arise from several levels, known or unknown, they always define our experience.

We can sense that with every choice we make, we are strengthening or weakening something, as well as receiving from it. For example, someone who chooses to smoke stimulates the tobacco industry and the effects on the world and people's health, just like drinking alcohol stimulates the alcohol industry and its effects on families, people, and the world. Who else could be the cause? Naturally, there're differences in the way people choose to use a substance when they do, but ultimately, we're all subject to the reality of influence. Since we are free, it is not a question of right or wrong, but of the existence of results and influences, which go beyond what we think we know. As long as people are serving as an example to start smoking, drinking, eating (or any other addiction), each one of us will have to decide how we want to be an example in that sphere of action, as in all others.

Since these are ingrained habits, many people feel like they do not know how to stop when they want to. Human beings can stop themselves from doing what they do not want to do anymore, at any time. If we only knew the decision-making power we possess, we would never hesitate. Most of the time, the greatest obstacle to freeing ourselves from addiction is not just its physical component, though this is the belief, but the entire structure created mentally and socially, and repeatedly accepted. In addition, there is this inner struggle of dealing with the difficulty of change, and it often is. However, there is no pressure, or even hurry; all change is determined by us at the inner level achieved by our will. We can discover habits that are truly good for us that are connected to our creativity and authenticity —unlike those we just copy from each other, helping us free ourselves from ties that have hurt us for so long.

First, you have to be able to see yourself beyond the roadblocks to free yourself from addiction. One of the effects of addiction is that it masks suffering, an artifice elected to reject it and make you unconscious of it, to keep it from rising to the surface, at least for a while. If we were to look at a specific case of a person whose addiction leads to external violence and multiple forms of aggression, we would probably be moved to compassion, since we would see proof of the old adage that "violence begets violence", demonstrating that behind a story there are always origins.

What can drive someone to inhale dense, foul-smelling smoke? It muddies the chest cavity, but before that, deep down, we see anxiety momentarily dimming existence. As an analogy, if we do not enjoy wearing excessive clothing every day, we might not live in cold climates. Were we to take off our clothes in a chilly environment, we would surely put them on again right away because the cold creates that temporary need. Smoking is similar because when you try to quit in the middle of a bout of anxiety, that contradictory needful desire returns — like you putting your clothes back on because of the cold. If we did not want to wear too much clothing, we would move from a hostile to a homeostatic climate beneficial to human beings. In the same way, as for smoking, we would exchange longing for beautiful contemplation.

Being against an addiction can provoke the same reaction from when we put ourselves against anything else, that is, we foment what we fight against to react once more. Therefore, there is no reason to be against the use of substances, for we may instead perceive that all kinds of sensations and states of consciousness experienced by the use of substances are naturally belonging to the individual himself, internal states attainable by being. *The essence of what is sought in the use of an external element is already available, even before, in each one of us.*

It may not be possible to discuss every kind of addiction here – the list would be too long; however, after observing more visible external habits, like those related to substance use, we can start observing the habits that become camouflaged by their conditions, such as addictive thoughts and feelings. On innumerable scales, we frequently see inter-obsession between people holding fixed thoughts, judgments, criticisms, or flattering each other in their minds. From feelings of rejection and low self-esteem to irritation and jealousy, we see that the repetitive patterns that constitute addiction also operate on these subtler levels, having the same origins as those of external order, demonstrating that every form of energy is rooted in love or fear. We can observe addiction to competition instilled in human habits everywhere from the educational environments all the way to the professional world. In the same way, lasciviousness stimulates promiscuity through an unwholesome focus on one of God's most beautiful gifts, namely sex, distorting this blessed opportunity for relationship. The world has struggled to make sex its driving force, and it has succeeded. Love embraces it because, after all, it is all that exists.

That being so, our responsibility is evident when we sense that, far from being isolated, our mental and emotional attitude influence all spheres of a shared world. Our attention is energy and nourishment; we can use it in the best conceivable ways. Therefore, the possibility of change is always within reach for those who are open to it, in a Universe that supplies everything necessary to facilitate each person's opening, reciprocating our decisions since whatever we truly choose is always given to us.

If we buy something in a bakery, we give a job to the baker; by talking to a child, we pass on a way of seeing the world; by buying a product, we incentivize its production; and by thinking or saying something about someone, we stimulate it in that person as well as in ourselves. Caring about something can become painful when it ceases to be a conscious choice (for the purpose chosen at the time) and becomes a mental need associated with any kind of attachment.

The "needs" expressed by a being always find resonance with the Love existing in the Universe. Quite often, the *illusion* of loneliness exists only in the mind. If we only knew how much love each person receives every moment, we would never doubt. After all, the great reason for existence is choosing to live what has been, is, and always will be the purposes of the spirit. It lacks the understanding that while it is something individual, those with affinities assist each other on an infinite scale. Caring about yourself is the best way to establish these higher goals. The effort involved in manifesting love when a being thirsts for it may seem contradictory, but the law of attraction is proven at every moment. Questioning life does not give you the answers through which beings find harmony, but by questioning what you are doing with *this opportunity*, you will always find a solution. Everything that exists is the result of the will, within inexhaustible options that are always respected. In the game of life, you can change it as you see fit. The greatest gift of the Creator.

Imagine the following: we put you in a house where you are going to spend some vacation time. Then we tell you a story about your experience in the house. While you are there, we state that the place is like a prison, from where it is unlikely you will leave unscathed. Anybody who stayed there did not fare well since it awakened the worst in them. It is always dusty and gets dirty easily; besides, you will most likely go hungry because there is no food in the house. Hearing this, you might become upset, angry, or fearful, spiral into depression or something similar. You might even feel distressed. However, if we put you in the same house, at the same address, and told you a different story, everything might turn out differently. If we said you were free to use it and do anything you want, that the house has suited everyone who has stayed there before very well, filling them with complete peace, awakening the best in them. Furthermore, we tell you that it is clean and well maintained, with everything you need. You would certainly have a different reaction and experience in that environment, would you not?

The point is that even though it is the same house, your mind placed you in different houses the moment you attached importance (or not) to the concepts presented to you. Some people's beliefs have been so influenced by suggestions that even if we told them a wonderful story about the house of life, they would not believe us. These people have lent so much importance to conflicting stories that accepting innovative proposals seems impossible. But it only seems that way. Although they may be easy to persuade and influence, the chosen beliefs are the greatest human power.

If we described to you a marvelous house and, upon arrival, you still found yourself in an environment apparently hostile and distant, worlds away from our description, you would be left with a few options. You could give up on your vacation and go home; or stay in the house despite the unpleasant and hostile characteristics; or even better, you could choose not only to stay but also get inspired by the pleasant description and transform it into a place of splendor, as great as or even better than our depiction.

The mind alters all our experiences without exception. This is what we have done with each other since birth, retelling stories about the "house of life." For example, life is full of villains and is very hard; everyone is born a sinner and guilty from birth; we live in a kind of prison; people do not get along, with themselves or with each other; we may go hungry sometime in our lives; and we must fight others, compete, and win to achieve what we want. Our minds will likely become upset, angry, or fearful, become despairing, disgusted or the like. However, it does not need to be this way. If we still see some situations like these in our own lives, it is just a temporarily condition in us, not permanent. They are creations of our minds/bodies/emotions. Human experience corresponds directly and indirectly to the beliefs that created them. The difference among human beings goes beyond the diverse influences to which they were exposed, but specially the beliefs stemming from these influences, causing reactions in each person, depending on what was absorbed or not (from those and other stories). Additionally, these beings deal with the influence of their own old tendencies.

And if we started telling a different story? What if we propagated the idea that we are free and can know ourselves; that an essential nature is always available to us internally. The idea that if we first make peace with ourselves, we will do better with others and that the Earth's abundance is enough for everybody and we can all share it intelligently and lovingly. Moreover, we would use this intelligence more efficiently if we realized that if every human being protects everybody else, in the end, we would all be protected. What would it be like if our stories were to tell that we have the power to lend importance to the best in each human being? What if we truly believe that a world renewed in love is possible?

God has placed us in the same life, yet our minds have put us in separate ones. Now it is up to us to choose which story we want to tell and which story we want to live.

# CHAPTER 9

Human beings have the dazzling and little-understood ability to believe. Though susceptible to the information surrounding them, they can choose whether to give power to each detail with which they are presented. To believe or not to believe, that is the question. Human minds have asked this question for millennia. But despite having this faculty, generally, individuals are still uncertain about how to use it. Experience is one of the greatest sources of information and awareness available to human beings, supplying every person with its living material. Still, most of us do not believe in the rich content of our own experiences; truly observing them. We prefer going along with other people's opinions, holding onto culturally pre-established ideas about their meaning. Feeling, clearly perceived in its truth, is one of the best ways for a person to know how to choose in any situation. Still, most of us do not believe in our own feelings and just react to the feelings of others. You are one of the gifts of nature. Yet, how many of us truly believe in ourselves? Why do we face so many internal difficulties as human beings? We believe in ourselves to the extent we know ourselves, just as we only see light in others as we see it internally. Let us know what is unknown to us about our own being to prepare ourselves better to perform this work with love.

For millennia, many people have only believed what the majority believed. They tend to think: "If everybody is doing something, so will I." Lacking the understanding that every conscience in the Universe unites with others in similar states, forming more or less direct relationships. Therefore, human civilization finds itself in relatively similar states of unconsciousness, until they no longer do, as more and more people awaken, as has been the case. They do not imagine how many spirits throughout the universe are constantly moving closer to love.

Ceasing to believe in yourself (as the flow of life) and basing your beliefs exclusively on what you have heard, will never bring you confidence. All this social frustration is no accident. We know where to find confidence in others as soon as we find our own. What is still happening among the majority of us is that very few know how to believe in ourselves. We often confuse such an achievement with the idea that we should trust on our own "I" as if the "I" was the same as the beliefs that inhabit our minds, which are mostly a blend obtained from the collective. In other words, how can I trust myself if I do not know who I am?

Day after day, in their many relationships, human beings are still trying to find their own confidence in others. They look for self-confidence in authorities, corporations, status, nations, money, intellectual knowledge, close friends or lovers, religion, science and other social structures. Above all, people still feel insecure on the inside. It happens because they seek self-confidence where there is none, since, in these cases, the other person is also looking for it because they lack it. It is like the blind leading the blind, or a deaf person asking another one about the best song to listen to.

True self-confidence is beyond everything. It is in the integration of the Being with Life and the eternity of the Being where nothing is threatened. The Being cannot be destroyed, only its form can and will perish sooner or later. In truth, trusting yourself is not the same as trusting exclusively in your own individuality; it means trusting the Life that is in everything, flowing through you and everyone. You experience death because you lose the self-image of this existence, but the Being is beyond any image. There is a space within you that is naturally full and secure, in peace and in the presence of the spirit. When the present moment seems unsatisfactory or graceless, or we are resisting it, it is because we are not entirely present in the now, in the miracle of life, but are mentally attached to the belief that we need something, generating some type of insecurity.

Love is the unmitigated source of security that all beings will come to recognize. There is a depth not seen by the eyes and barely reached by thought. Such inspiration is revealed when the veils that distort perception are removed. We have all interacted with someone for whom love comes from within. Even those who have chosen to live an existence amid what they call perversity have had experiences that called them to love, although they may temporarily hide them out of fear, not risking immersion in this inexhaustible source. Even though the people for whom we cultivate this sentiment may not be physically present, love remains present in us. Many people forget this small detail. Nothing can take away the love that lives inside you; only you can continue moving away from it. By the same token, although we may remember each other, only you can move closer again.

Life's singularity is brilliant, filling each existential moment with meaning. *Death exists so we may see life.* The "you" that everyone knows is unique. Nobody will ever see a "John" or a "Mary" like the ones who are here right now. The mark of that existence will always be unique. Although we all move through eternal Life, transforming ourselves through the moments of time, reincarnation allows us to perceive the singularity of this existence by seeing ourselves and our loved ones in a temporary, finite state. No specific belief or mental understanding is necessary about reincarnation for the spirit to manifest its fullness, yet the eternal dance of the being through life and death happens similar to the heart that beats with or without our understanding.

How many of us have been through the experience of seeing someone we love leaving the flesh through the death of the body? How many have felt someone's breathing fade away? How many have touched a cold body that has ceased generating their intense light? Practically everyone has gone or will go through an experience like this. How often do people regret the choices they made regarding their loved ones after they depart? Perhaps they think they could have done something different or done it better.

Happy are those who know they can do better now, that there is always a path. We do not need to wait for our loved ones to depart (they all will, although meeting again is possible) for us to become aware of the value of their presence each time we meet. It does not need to be this way. Every spirit draws to itself compatible company; fortunate are those who become compatible with the union of God, where everyone is a correspondent of love.

There is no reason to spend our lives running away from people, society or life; there is no need to struggle to survive. The survival of the spirit has always been guaranteed. Do not worry so much about tomorrow –every day is today. Today is the tomorrow that will be called now. The physical form of these and other things as we know them will perish. At any time, the person in front of us may disappear in the next moment. All manifestations of property originate from the human illusion. Nobody belongs to anybody. No attachment is truly binding. The first thing you should know when someone enters your life is that at one time or another, you or they will depart. That is the gift of the infinity of experiences, the uniqueness of each one. Only one thing feels eternal and does not perish: love, and the presence you cultivated in yourself and that you leave to those who want to enjoy it. Do enjoy it.

Life is made of choices, happy of those who are aware of them. Do not be afraid of loving and being loved since any fear is merely the absence of love. Make the decision to choose consciously. Life proposes to you that you fully embrace it wherever you go. That is the only choice you never need to postpone—to love always, here and now. Each new meeting is an opportunity to bring your truth. Every situation is a chance to bring your peace. Each episode is an occasion to bring life. Every occurrence on your journey is free in and of itself, so liberate yourself. Each moment is an opportunity to make the excellent choice to love. There is no boredom or scarcity in the act of love. Although the form may appear the same to dull eyes, those who cultivate the state of love will perceive and taste this treasure that belongs to everyone, transcending appearances. Sharing between individuals knows no limits, except the ones we establish. Love is the power to renew everything and to make everything eternal. But, how do we go beyond the established limits?

Commonly, individuals come to *identify* themselves with something, with a constructed image, telling themselves: "This is me." People identify with all sorts of things, conforming to those roles with a degree of unconsciousness, as fathers, mothers, spouses, blood relatives, teachers, educators, students, or professionals, as belonging to a country or culture, even as fans of sports teams, among many other examples. If this is the case, you probably do it more often than you realize. The mind is a brush painting the picture we call reality.

Every suffering comes from identification with a story, a personal image. Which stories do you defend? Which ones do you attack, so they will continue conforming to yours? In this struggle, everyone loses. We create our own narrative in the meandering of our mind until it is contested by experience, generating suffering. Unlike physical pain, which often results naturally from other incidents such as a broken bone, the pain caused by suffering is generated by a more relative context. Even organic pain can be perceived without additional suffering, when surrender and integration stand before the spirit beyond the physical form, where you cannot be frightened.

What image do you have of yourself? Many fear not having any at all. If I don't have an image to present to others, then who am I? That would be the question to ask. Generally, without knowing it, we fear not having one, since we normally believe that unless we identify with the models of the "I," we will remain alone, feeling lonely or empty. However, there are those who spend their lives conforming to certain roles and still feel incomplete and alone. A clear sign of self-sabotage. How often have we renounced the cultivation of our fullest states of presence to piously conform to a self-image? How often have we renounced getting to know inherent states of our being, confused by the predominant collective thoughts? Many people perceive and question some of these roles in society; however, creating mechanisms based on pride to deny or confront them, thus maintaining an intense connection to these images, instead of freeing themselves from them. Human figures and representations need not be denied or repudiated, they can be transcended. In other words, we can move beyond what they represent. In a way, as we try to free ourselves from images about ourselves, exercising caution can be prudent to avoid creating a reinforced image of someone who has none, trying, almost in vain, to grasp this neutral position in our mind. Obviously, images will exist in your mind, just do not identify yourself specifically with any of them.

Not a single one defines who you are; at most, they may define how you are momentarily. Therefore, you do not move beyond representations by denying, remaining neutral or empty, but rather, by not limiting yourself, overcoming them. Effectively detaching oneself only means no longer having a fixed, well-defined or definitive image, leading the flexibility of your being with freedom and naturalness. The essence of Life in any being cannot be defined by images or concepts, since it simply is. There is no single definition of who we are; however, we define and redefine ourselves through experience every single moment.

Concepts do not define us in essence. Nevertheless, each moment of your experience is a temporary definition of who you are choosing to be here and now. In the end, you are always the one who generates your life's affirmations in the experience, so that consciously defining your experience is an act of freedom, through the expression of who you choose to be at any given moment. The conceptual definition of oneself is always incomplete, while the experimental definition is the manifestation of who you choose to be at every instant. So, at this point, the question is, how do I choose to experience myself now? The universe behind how you feel is a result of how you are choosing to define yourself in that moment. Yet the fullness of Being is beyond any concepts, or even experiences, for it is our inherent nature.

Which behaviors are you used to accepting as "yours?" When we think we have previously experienced something identical to what is occurring now, it is our mind finding a model to fit our experience, trying to repeat it in a false idea of security. There might be patterns and similarities, however, there is always something unique about the moment to be observed and harnessed by the spirit. Conscious malleability is one of the natural conditions of the being.

As long as we expect praise to strengthen our self-image, we are affected in the same way by criticism since, in our minds, they both arrive via the same route. Praise and criticism are part of the human condition. Not needing either is the fundamental transformation, but when they do occur, we can merely observe them, absorbing what is valid. The hardest part is when praise and criticism become the criteria most of us choose in our circle of relationships, depriving beings of the characteristics of their personalities, who become embarrassed to be the subject-matter of the day. The line between approval, criticism and honest sharing is very thin.

Living life is like writing a book. You are not going to write it based on the thoughts and judgments of others. If you did, you would never get past the first line without thousands of external contradictions and influences distorting the unfolding of your sentence. It is not unlike living a full life, for your writing to flow you need to disconnect yourself from the expectations of other people's reactions and connect yourself to the light of the present moment, allowing inspiration, intuition and insight to move through you.

Every image is superficial, like the tip of an iceberg. The form is like an information portal; beyond it is an entire universe to be uncovered. People who typify their "I" with representations tend to see any form solely by its appearance, according to what they see. By going beyond this, in accord with the being, a kind of portal opens before each image, a field of unlimited information, through which one can go across to know more closely and deeply the truth and presence expressed in this field.

As examples, when human beings light a candle, gaze at someone's physical body, or read a book, they normally see the superficial form each of those circumstances conveys. As they go even further into the vivacity of their being, they increasingly see not only the lit candle but also the field provided by faith, intention and energy that can use the candle as an instrument, although it may not be necessary. Little by little, they no longer see only the appearance of the human form before them, but the content, the context of the being and information carried by that person in that moment. Gradually, they no longer see only concepts, phrases and ideas in writings and books, analyzing them according to others they acquired previously; rather, they feel whatever truth there is in those words that can touch their experience. Truly seeing something beyond form is only possible insofar as it is done in oneself. From there on, we might be able to leave the mind, which is like a restrictive box and go beyond; going beyond is like leaving a closed house and taking a walk through a beautiful park. Considering the beyond is infinite, there is so much more to experience, the possibilities are abundant.

Paying attention is an act of pure love. It is no accident that one of fear's main characteristics is to run away from the object of fear, to look away from what is frightening. Attention is the being's natural ability to love with its presence. The excess of concepts and paradigms limits and alters the level of energy released by our attention. When we deconstruct paradigms, the field is cleared, and love frees itself through pure attention. When we observe someone beyond the image they present, it is possible for us to feel their consciousness, alive, and when we feel someone else's consciousness, we feel ourselves. That is one facet of what we call love.

The images people have become used to cultivating for themselves — for a limited perception of time and space — will fade away at death. However, other perceptions of the "I" will then emerge, indefinitely and continuously, like an expanding fractal. We are increasingly becoming aware of our respective assumed roles, learning a little more about what is beyond them, like a child who seeing through the window the first few times, begins to see the landscape of the world. Drawing nearer to the consciousness of the eternal being opens a range of possibilities for the spirit. Instead of merely playing social roles, the multiplicity of being is now addressed in consciousness. In truth, every individual can state: there is as much in heaven, as on earth, as there is in me.

There is a different way of dealing with situations, by seeing each moment that was once considered perturbing as an opportunity to better know and work on ourselves spiritually, here and now. If you believe that you no longer need to know about yourself, your mind will position itself to wait for the day when the inner work is done, the day when you no longer need to pay attention to yourself. But that day does not exist, since we are infinite beings, and everything changes moment by moment, in impermanence. At the same time, there is no rush or pressure nor is there anything for you to "work" on, in the best sense of that word, which is not in the present. If you treat every one of your moments as one of these opportunities, whenever they arise, you will not condemn them, but use them as opportunities to know yourself and set aside your anguish in exchange for the feats of life's transformations. Soon you will perceive spirit acting on the screen of your consciousness, presenting an array of aspects of your being, unfolding one element of unconsciousness at a time, one by one the multiple facets of your being are revealed, each at the right moment.

Several walks of society encourage people to find their identity. Nevertheless, most human beings find themselves in conflict with their identity, with who they think they are. They try to shape their personalities according to "subliminal agreements" about who they are. They then strive to do something to be in agreement with those beliefs. Which ideas agree with whom you believe yourself to be? Self-esteem problems only exist when we believe in a self-image to be esteemed. Identity is what determines the sense of "I." Nevertheless, while human beings identify with something exclusively, there are others doing the same with different conceptions about who they are, and this causes separation between their minds. Bloody wars, fights between two or thousands of people, or arguments in the mental space itself, all originate from this cause. It is beneficial for the myriad human differences to continue to exist; all the same, without being tied to a single one of them and being against the others, but because they are clearly connected, we embrace one another. One cannot skillfully define the "I," it just is. This might sound surprising considering social concepts, but we are saying there may not be a defined identity. We are free and flowing beings. If some kind of inherent identity does exist, it is the one connected to everything that is, transcending any sense of a mental "I." Instead of spending our lives incessantly searching for a self-identity, may we see it is, always has been and will be here, in the Life that we are. In that case, we can move through all cultural identities, for example, without limiting ourselves to them, but instead seeing the essence of being behind those forms.

People frequently confuse *being* with *doing*. When you do not know who you are, you do something to try and discover it. What do you do? Perhaps you do what others asked, showed, demanded of you, or have done themselves. You will probably base what you do every day on what your parents, teachers, friends, acquaintances, celebrities and other people have done. Unless you are, before you do.

What we will see is that we are not what we have done with each other! Nothing we have told, taught and shown each other for eons defines who we are in essence. Each belief that has been demonstrated to us, even before a birth, or each time we were babies, each class in school or lesson from our parents, each conversation with friends or strangers, each TV show or book we read, none of these have ever fully defined who we are. All of these things result from what we have done toward others, how much we have influenced each other, whether considered good or bad. Regardless of what was done, on levels closest to the essence everything was allowed by all those involved, in such a way that not a single piece is out of place. Therefore, there is nothing they have done to you that is not part of a greater scope, where everything is in accordance with free-will and the spiritual path of all involved in the experience. Even so, what was done does *not define* who you are. And who are you now? The aspect of who you truly are that you choose to be. In human civilization, there is still a disparity between doing and being. In Spirituality, those two elements turn into the same thing.

If what they did to you hurt you, remember: at this moment, you do not remember who you are in the face of that detail. There is no problem with that. You are rediscovering it. Accepting our internal situation with humility is always better when surrendering ourselves to a new understanding. If there is a part of you still hurting, there is an aspect of yourself that has not been acknowledged. Why is this? Because who you really are cannot be hurt. Only self-images get hurt when they are not reciprocated. We all are part of the Universe, of God's perfect system, of the light spectrum that vibrates in infinity, of the dust of stars. And darkness? It does not exist on its own; it only happens so we may see light illuminate, just like we need a canvas on which to paint colors. And so, its essence in its most sublime perspective is perfect. There are no problems, hurts or fears in your soul. Rather the soul wanted to see its light in the experience, subjecting itself to its laws. Every soul wanted that. It is the reason why under certain circumstances, God/Life can seem irrelevant to everyone, like it does not care and lets things stay the way they are. It is only appearances; the way it seems to be, and it does not define what is.

Imagine the following scene, putting ourselves in the role of father or mother. Parent-child relationships can be metaphorically compared to the relationship between God and all of us. Children generally possess a curious disposition, asking their parents and close ones all kinds of questions. Some of the answers cannot yet be understood deeply by children at such tender age such as sexuality, how children are born, events in the professional world, among other things. Their parents try to explain as much as possible in accordance with their stage of development, in a simplified, introductory, romantic, or metaphorical manner, sometimes temporarily omitting information until the children develop the conditions to understand. It takes years to children understand certain details in greater depth. The relationship human beings have with God is similar in this matter. If a child takes years to learn what their parents and teachers have to share with them, just imagine how much time the Universe has to demonstrate all of its mysteries, enigmas and laws to spirits. For that, we have the eternal present moment. If the difference in understanding between children and adults is already considerable, imagine the difference between the entire Universe and human conditions. Our advantage is that God is and lives in each of us and vice versa, and so, the effect is precise.

There is no way to present all of God's enigmas to the spirit with immediacy. It would be the end of the fun. Therefore, may we have keen intent, but be well accompanied by virtuous patience. May we have humbleness before life. It is no accident we have eternity supporting us. Recognizing each person's momentary state, as well as the existence of incommensurable surroundings around all of us, in far-away lands, unknown worlds, extraordinary stars and different dimensions — all still superficial details within God's relevance and depth — is always advantageous for the being. Just as children experiment with life, expanding and developing their capacity to understand certain subjects, every spirit does the same throughout eternity, in an incalculable portion of possibilities and experiences.

We have an entire Universe surrendering itself to us, allowing us to surrender ourselves, here within and without, as one. The system is perfect, even though you may not see it. The result is certain, the only absolute certainty since it is always here. We have all eternity to be ourselves. How are we going to be?

We are only what we are when we had not been what we are. To know itself, our light has known darkness. We understand more about who we are when we come to understand who we are not. Many are the spirits who still seek to be who they are not until they discover new truths. How frequently they immerse themselves in darkness in revolt. Many like drama, as long as this is the case, it will always be respected within the workings of the Universe. But the time always comes, there is no hurry in the process, and the fun is in the journey. As spirits, we are examining the grounds, preparing the canvas so we can bring in more and more colors to paint it. This game, in the good sense of the word, is an agreement among all of us, among all souls. We temporarily forget on some levels, but we are all playing, all living. There is no greater proof of love among beings, all of us surrendering ourselves to a living game, and while some forget, others come to remember, and vice versa.

What have they done to you? That is a question you can ask yourself. When you come to know, remember, do not lend importance to what they did to you, or take it as yours, if you do not want to. Whoever it is and whatever it was, was secretly expecting you would show who you really are. Darkness always wants to see light, even if only to deny it.

There is something else to know. Who are you not? For you to be yourself, you go through what you are not, then what you are not is also a part of what you are. Everything is in the process of eternity. Therefore, choose. Decide what to be in the amplitude of the Universe. If you have the intention of remembering yourself and everyone else, as others have done and are doing – within the game we are living so we can play it better and better – do it by being. You are all of us, and all of us are you. Open your path, be life. Open your mind, be truth. Open your feelings, be love. Open your ego, be humility. Who you are will be all these things. Never mind those who do not listen to you, see you, or even try to hurt you. Remember, we have all agreed to this since forever, and everything is an eternal passage. The time will come for them to remember, and so will yours. When that happens, take your steps, become action and say to whoever wants to listen: let us go together.

# CHAPTER 10

I t is a joy when we become aware of our own body as an instrument worthy of creation, that one day will return to where it emerged from, serving as food for plants, animals, and beings that used to nourish us. The body is its own expression, an element of experience that can be honored with your way of living. The consciousness that leaves a body with gratitude and respect glorifies that instrument of form. In fact, our body is being renewed each and every moment, undergoing constant transformation.

Individuals tend to imprint patterns that mold their body. There are individual and collective models. Your physical constitution is not defined by a genetic coincidence related to your parents, but by an entire set of circumstances related to choices of the spirit facing incarnation. Parents, and their characteristics, provide options for those choices and are also part of this aggregate. Its physical form is a somatic result of entirely interconnected spiritual, mental, emotional and physical information that molds this sacred mechanism.

Every image that you have of yourself influences and can limit your body through programmed and established ideas, either of criticism or praise. Your self image tends to change constantly over the course of your existence, as does your physical organism. Behind the form is a constant and inherent presence no image can contain. For those whose eyes are open, they discern the luminosity of spirit that emanates beyond the form. The face and the gaze are the points of the body that come closest to showing the luminosity of the spiritual presence.

All self-definition directly interferes with the body's functioning at every moment. *The mind is to the body as climate is to plants.* Without mental restrictions, we accept our corporeal instrument as it is, and at the same time we become conscious of its experience so that light and beauty naturally flow into our perception, balancing the "mental climate" to refine the body for the purpose of the spirit.

While the body is a fully intelligent complex, contrary to popular belief, it is not a self-contained intelligent organism, as an isolated form, since, when confronted with death, its organization is disfigured, with no ability to maintain itself independently, returning to the intelligence and life on Earth. Nor does the intelligence that organizes the body come from the mind (which influences and participates in it), since it is not necessary to think about its complex nature. The intelligence that organizes form comes from the beyond, from the formless. In the case of an individual's body, through the spirit.

The spiritual garment is not adorned with trappings such as cotton, silk or any of the materials commonly used in body clothing; but rather, it is made of energy. The spiritual garment is pure energetic expression, so that while two people can wear the same clothes, they will each give different impressions. The garment of the spirit adorns them more than any other ornamentation, revealing sometimes more and sometimes less of the brilliance of their being, through subtle means.

There is no such thing as an isolated body. Physically, bodies are composed of multiple organisms in circulation with the world around them, just like a variety of bacteria and microorganisms. Even the body's atoms came from the formation of stars, billions of years ago. The intelligence we see in form — plants, animals, humans, planets, stars, and other unimaginable configurations across the universe — does not have true points of separation, it is but one. Now there is something that could be reevaluated by the scientists who developed the theory of the origin of life. Life has always been present, since everything is Life in movement. The concept of life, if reevaluated for our New Times, demonstrates that it is not only found within the limits established by researchers, through convention, but that life is movement itself. Vibration. Our naked eyes can see animals changing and plants growing, but rocks, for example, don't they change their shape over time? We know that rocks appear motionless, but if you use a microscope you can see their molecules and atoms in constant motion, and their subtle energy is in circulation as well. If we need classification, we can at most make the relative differentiation between what they consider organic and inorganic, as merely being different degrees of evolution and manifestation of life. Vegetable, animal and human bodies all need minerals to provide vitality, do they not?

Happy are the children who see Life in everything, just as those who make themselves as lively as children are happy. Life is the vibration of energy, undergoing transformations at all times. So that the Universe may expand and move energy, instead of everything being in absolute disarray in the cosmos, it organizes its forms intelligently, like the structuring of a simple plant or the planets in a galaxy, disorganizing them at times while promoting arrangements of new vibrant forms.

Is not what we call death only perception changing references? In other words, what happens when you die? You live. There is only Life in constant transformation, in myriad manifestations from dense to subtle that can scarcely be imagined.

What soil is most alive? The best fertilizer is full of elements considered dead, in decomposition. Soil is only "infertile" when there was not enough diversity of beings for their structures to die and share their physical vitality. Still, different existential forms grow in even the most inhospitable environments. Death is only life changing form, continuing in the vibration that sings behind every movement. Is death the end of life? For consciousness, it is not. It is only existence changing its course. There is no death, just something in mutation, there is no end, only the end of the way things look, while life goes on in constant transformation. Fertile soil is the self-renewing kind that overflows with life when death occurs. For eyes that see, everything is Alive in its own way.

Do you want to conserve your life? Preserving it would be to lose it as you know it. You cannot place an existence into a cast, nor immobilize an appearance or a situation, you cannot conserve a definite form. Wanting to hold onto your life is the same as going against it. Wanting to stop your transformation is the same as cloistering a rose. In your attempt to preserve and capture it, you place the rose in a separate place — it loses its charm as it wilts in solitude. While free, the rose lives fully, touched by the sun and bathed in the rain, blossoming and withering among its sisters that come and go. While the rosebush was there, a hummingbird came by one day for a kiss, and the rose was fully realized. Then its form fell to earth, and its scent went to heaven, and now it goes on.

People have been living like roses who believe they are independent from the rosebush. Look at a tree rose. Its seed is the seedling. Its seedling is the stem. Its stem is the trunk. Its trunk is the limb. Its limbs are the branches. The branches are the roses. The rose is the entire tree. The form of the rose may go away, but its essence remains on the rosebush, so new flowers may be born.

Fear of death is rather a fear of life. Avoiding death in an attempt to preserve life, grasping its form, is like the rose escaping the rosebush to become an artificial, plastic flower. Your body transforms itself over time, cells die and are renewed. You do not have the same body throughout your existence; you reincarnate from moment to moment. Like the rose that solidified, each locked up emotion, each limiting thought, and each intention that separates you hinders your body from being reborn naturally. A repressed, sublimated emotion does more harm to the body than spoiled food. A healthy body cleanses itself after eating spoiled food, but an energetically blocked body attacks itself.

In fact, your organism has a perfect immune system. A well-balanced immune system is truly immune. What we know as pathology or any other imbalance in a body, becomes necessary because on some more subtle level the individual chose it. The vast majority of times, this is not a direct choice, rather the result of deep, oftentimes unconscious choices. A sick body is the result of some infirmity in that person as a being. There is no reason to avoid it, since illness is a normal part of the human process, at least for now. There are individuals with a broadly developed consciousness who experience illness, since the effects of their choices run on another timescale. Nor does every healthy body mean a healthy individual as a whole, for illness only emerges at the moment the spirit chooses as appropriate for the expansion of consciousness. Illness is just another path towards healing, towards self-knowledge. If you make it necessary, the imbalance will grab your attention, developing your self-perception towards whatever generated it. Oftentimes it will concern aspects of your way of life, or more specifically, how your inner self has dealt with it. Every illness and imbalance have a reason and an origin, they manifest themselves as a call for you to perceive what needs to be transformed.

Through experience, illness can lead to health, by a different path from which health leads to health. Likewise, imbalance can bring you towards equilibrium, as well as balance. Health is never represented by a certain appearance deemed socially appropriate for the physical body, but rather through the being's vitality as a whole. What these experiences provide us with is an opportunity to know aspects of who we are not, while our own perception reemerges, finding ourselves as our essence emerges. On a deep level, you need do nothing more than clearly see what the illness or imbalance has brought you. Self-awareness is the best nourishment, the source of healing for the body. We only need to perceive what is perceivable; so, what is truly necessary will come into our experience, after all, everything comes from the choice of the spirit.

Look at yourself, truly meditate on your imbalance, or even better, on what balances you. Look at yourself in the mirror and be thankful for the ability to see its causes and effects, on each of the levels they present themselves. Your body and the complexity of your senses, like your sentiments and thoughts, are blessings of your experience so that you may know yourself. Observe, through the light of your consciousness, the intense movement of life.

Behind all existence is movement. Perceiving the circulation behind things is a key to enlightened perception. Everything is continuously moving, even what appears immobile. What we tend to label as immobile does not, in fact, exist in that state. The state of immobility is only apparent. We see a motionless object in front of us, and when we are perceptually limited to the form's appearance, we think it is not moving. Even solid objects, which seem so hard, are in constant transformation. On an atomic level, they are always changing. The energy that makes the objects exist is moving. Everything created in the universal nature has not remained the same, not even the most solid forms, which are transformed in constant storms.

This enlightened perception occurs through a state of contemplation, silent observation. People have a habit of seeing the forms around them — people, objects, or other beings — through the images they have learned about them. They don't exactly see what is in front of them, only what their minds have learned about what is there. Simply perceive without putting anything into what you observe, let what is observed show itself to you. See without setting a previous vision on top of the present one. Listen without setting a previous sound on top of the current one. Feel without setting a previous sentiment on top of the current one. See, hear and feel what is in your present moment. Your essence cannot be threatened by whatever surrounds you since you are all of it. May we cultivate our bodies for life as it is, rather than what we have been told it has to be.

Everything that comes across our path has its own story, a context, that can be observed and felt. Every detail in the Universe has made its own journey to arrive where it is. It is like a conversation: if you only want to speak, you cannot listen to what others have to say, you cannot learn more about them, your Life companions. We are all traveling together through life. We can listen to nature and all the elements surrounding us. There is a dance all around us. A dance of the essence of who we are. See the essence in all presences, and you will see them dancing. When birds fly through the sky, see that essence dancing around you through the air. When you look at a flower, note that its essence has danced through rain, earth, sap and branches of the plant creating eye-catching blooms. When you come face-to-face with a person, see both the context of their existence and the dance of their conscience through eternity. That enlightened perception is reflected in the observance of a natural flow that is always present.

Usually, we believe that human beings are capable of doing what their physical structure allows them to do. Human genetics allows us to walk, run, think, and much more. Have you ever considered that everything we believe as possible for the human being shapes its structures, rather than the structures allowing what is possible?

Far back in the past, when human beings believed they had limited skills, they only accomplished what they thought possible. Genetics and brain structure are a materialization of beliefs that we established about ourselves, but mainly, of objectives of the spirit, as means to awaken consciousness. It is no coincidence that the human body has changed over the course of history, along with the development of its beliefs. Is walking on two feet and erect considered normal? The entire law of gravity was challenged for it to become possible. They were truly miraculous, those moments in which *we*, as those beings from millions of years ago, intuitively found that if we were able to walk upright, as bipeds, we could significantly increase our experiences. Until we understood that we could, truly believing, generating those experiences that came to make sense. Once we comprehended how much better we could use our hands and fingers, we developed countless skills. When we believed in our intellectual capacity, we created languages, inventions and technology. If we had not believed that we could walk, use our hands and our intellect, we would not have had these experiences, just like many others that remain as yet unknown. What will become of us when we believe in our spiritual capacity?

Everything in life is a miracle. From the simplest to the most complex principle. You want to move your arm and a perfect structure of life responds to your wish. By forgetting this, in some cases, physical structures sometimes cease to respond in a healthy manner, as if to remind them of this disregarded fact. Every detail of life possesses splendid, miraculous elements. The chemical, physical and biological dance in your body is glorious. Those feats beyond normal capabilities accomplished by those who transcend are considered miraculous, but few perceive that everything we do, everything we are is a miracle. When we sense this, loving ourselves and Life, other miracles we used to not understand also begin to reveal themselves naturally.

The human body is continually modified according to changes in beliefs and decisions. The physical body is made of countless energy channels traversing numerous paths on different levels, which together with their physical counterparts intelligently compose its experiential form. On our spiritual paths, the form does not need to be denied, only enlightened by consciousness. Taking responsibility for the body is also basic, aligning oneself to the stimulation of universal health.

If we take our observation to feel the energy in our bodies, we can look at it from the angle of two basic energies related to each other, forming three main centers. Although we could observe other several smaller ramifications, we have our eyes turned to a unified energetic field. Proceeding from the sky to the body, a subtler energy is found around the head, in a *higher center*, where the basis of all levels of the mind is constituted. There is a denser energy around the abdominal region that rises from the earth to the body, near the sexual organs, in a *lower center* where physical, sexual and creative energy forms. From the meeting of these two energies in a *middle center* around the chest arises the source of balance, from where love is expressed as everything that is beyond mind and matter.

The more the middle center comes into balance and full resonance, it expands as it crosses all the energy channels of the body and mind, connecting them in living and enlightened sentiments, transforming everything into a single energetic body. When we perceive our own energetic body, we verify through experience that it has no limits, that starting from itself it expands and unifies with everything.

These energies flow around each other constantly, from moment to moment, over the course of our experiences. Disharmony among them results in a relationship of extremes. For example, an overload of sexual energy in the lower center (when out of balance), results in a backlash to the upper center, changing the mental energy, creating oscillations. The same balancing can occur with so many other apparently distinct energies in us as individuals, which possess similar origins deep in our energetic body. Recognizing this energetic instability through sensitivity, by means of our perceptive instruments, is another step towards the emergence of consciousness. Soon, we no longer identify ourselves with the imbalance believing that it represents who we are. We merely contemplate it so we can then awaken spiritually. As we achieve mindfulness, the middle center naturally succeeds in manifesting its balancing function, transmuting old learned disharmonies through love, compassion, truth and joy. When this is fully realized, we feel our entire energetic body, and even though our legs may be walking, we are accompanied by a sensation of floating along with everything.

Besides the physical body, we use a mental body, composed of countless subtle forms. Thought has a magnetic force that needs our attention so that the thought process may continue. If that attention is accompanied by taking on a limiting identity for yourself, the mental will control your energy and you may become lost in thought. Nevertheless, if we contemplate our thoughts harmoniously, we can expand them to the excellence of love.

Allegorically, each thought is similar to an automobile. For it to move, it needs the fuel of our attention. Our mind creates drivers searching for cars to drive. When there is identification with a specific thought, the sense of "I" becomes tied to a specific idea about itself, and the driver of the mind becomes tied to a car with a specific route to follow. Since who we really are is not limited to a defined belief of ourselves, or to a single type of thought, there is a natural dissatisfied impulse in our being regarding our idea of ourselves, and of disgust regarding the route we have gotten stuck on. As a consequence, the mind tries to create a new driver in an attempt to drive elsewhere, using imagination to take new routes. However, many individuals habitually hold themselves to old ideas, or identify with them once again, disturbing the flow on their mental highways. The drivers created by the mind end up stuck in certain cars on specific routes (repetitive lines of thought). While this process reproduces itself, the mind insanely creates a massive contingent of drivers in search of vehicles to drive through a complex and biased system of jumbled up thoughts, since the drivers tend to follow the same routes using the same cars. For this reason, instead of flowing, the mind is stuck in a gigantic traffic jam — when it is not causing serious accidents. This mechanism creates the external realities of insanity that exist in our current society, where so many people feel trapped in their everyday lives, when in fact they have become trapped in their beliefs.

When you no longer identify with your thoughts, and you do not freeze your perception of "I" in a mold that creates a limited idea of your personality, you come to see the thoughts as a movement, a creative force. Now who you are can move freely through the vehicles of thought, traveling via these eminent instruments, every moment. On such occasion, you go beyond normal thought and observe yourself observing your thoughts, in a way, embracing this whole process consciously. Who you are is not conceptually definable, but moves through all of these existential vehicles like an infinite source, the spirit. If we limit who we are to a concrete idea of ourselves, some type of frustration will always remain, because an impulse of truth innate to us will strive to liberate us from the tie-ups we have created. If who we are is not limited to form (thought is also a form), there is no reason to identify with it, in the sense of ending our perception of "I" there. Form exists for the possibility of becoming conscious of what is beyond form, in other words, form is a projection of the formless and human existence a projection of the spirit, to expand consciousness.

When we understand that form is only a projection of the spirit, of the formless, and therefore, a transitory creation of the Being, we comprehend that because of this, who we are is also form, but without limiting ourselves to it. They are not separate; they are one. As we become conscious of this not only as an idea but as our experience, we become closer to the comprehension of God.

# CHAPTER 11

D o you understand that we — all Beings — are gods, as long as we are one? In fact, we create our entire reality, and for the most part, we still do this unconsciously, along with the rest of humanity and other forms of life. Regarding all things, our beliefs are revealed and/or transformed since whatever we believe in, deep in our thoughts, finds a way to manifest itself.

Let us look at three types of thoughts. Creative, sustaining, and destructive. Every thought is the fuel, to say the least, for finding others of the same sphere to join in a field of collective thoughts. Each thought can *destroy* something that was built, *sustain* something that was generated, or *create* something new. Essentially, each thought is creative, since it can also create destruction or re-create something, sustaining it for that moment. One of the greatest difficulties humans have faced in creating their reality has been the frequent oscillation between creative and destructive thoughts or, just as much, by unconsciously supporting ignoble contexts. It is not that every thought directly creates our reality, but basically, by its essence. What matters, most of the time, is not exactly the imagined form of thinking, but the essence and energy behind the type of thought, which lends substance to reality.

Words are an expression of thought. Each spoken word carries a certain type of energy. While two people can say the same sentence, it will not be the same. Each individual's sentence is uttered in accordance to the very being before it. Each term they articulate bears their truth upon expression. For this reason, it is pointless to merely change our words if an inner movement does not accompany the change. Each and every expression demonstrates this, in some way. Sooner or later, people will come to understand that, when we speak, our words are impregnated with a certain energy. Many are those who perceive the energy imbued in physical environments, altering the way we feel. In the same way, human beings are impregnated with vibrations of all kinds. Those who clearly observe this context in themselves gradually begin to generate speech that easily turns into action.

Thought usually manifests itself in two ways. The first one is what you could call *background thoughts*. Regardless of what we say, there is always a thought deep in our minds, conscious or not, which is what we really think about something. In other words, you might say what you think about a certain situation, but if what is in your mind's background is different, that is what counts towards creating your reality. We can even fool and deceive ourselves, but our mind does not fool the functioning of the Universe. That is the thought that directly influences occurrences. That is the chosen thought, the determining nature, the energy generator. The detail is that the choice does not always occur on a conscious level. Many individuals are in contradiction with their own thoughts, cultivating masks to cover the cellars of their own minds.

We may state something original that may shake a few, although it is simple for the oneness. Every thought about someone that is in the background of your mind, in other words, everything you really think about them, is always known by the spirit of the person to whom it is destined. There is a level on which the Being knows everything. In the current state of humanity, the vast majority are not conscious of this level. At most, we have an inkling of intuition and sensitivity. The more conscious we are, the more we become aware of the unexpected occurring behind what is said or demonstrated, even from a distance. If human beings were conscious of the many levels of interaction, they would make choices from a new perspective. Many correspond to what others think about them, even though they do not know what it is. Have your own light, see it in the other one, for in so doing you will be of aid to them.

The second way is what we can call *reiterated thought*. When a type of thought becomes a pattern, it finds a means of manifestation. This constancy makes it possible to gather sufficient energy, compatible with that type of thought, for it to express itself as action in the world. Indeed, the reiterated thought manifests itself because it is repeated so often that it is transformed into a constant thought in the background of the mind.

If thought A, B or C emerges in your mental environment, there is no reason to worry or blame yourself. Do not resist or identify with it, just observe it and let it pass. Become aware of its existence and surrender yourself, let go of whatever is not good enough for you and everyone else, thereby making room for many more clarifying and satisfactory thoughts. Next, choose which thought you lend your force and energy to, the one you intend to bring to the background of your mind. When you have chosen, assimilate it, apply it in your daily life in different contexts, at different times, reaching the repetition that turns thought into reality.

Thought is one human intellectual capability that could be utilized more advantageously. Nevertheless, if you think that you cannot stop thinking for a moment, your mind is fooling you. Thought is only a tiny fraction of our totality many others can emerge beyond the internal dialogue of the mind. Try to imagine how it would be to attempt to comprehend the world by using only one of your corporeal senses, such as through touch alone. Though you have the others available to you, they would soon fall into disuse. This is, in fact, what has occurred with human beings in general, living as they do, tied to an unconscious ego, limiting themselves to the mental reactions provoked by this instrument's programming, while many other unimaginable faculties lie dormant.

If touch were the only sense available for you to exercise your perception, whenever anyone tried to share something with you, surely they would do it in a way that you could comprehend, through touch, until it became possible to show you in another way. That is why we use words to address the understanding we bring here, so that they are first recognized on the level to which many of us are accustomed, that of thoughts, so that we can gradually share more experiences from sources beyond the mind. If someone tried to comprehend taste through touch, they would touch their lips, mouth and tongue, trying to familiarize themselves with that mechanism. If they were to try to comprehend touch through vision, they would look at their feet, hands, and skin, while leaning them against another surface, watching each one reaching the other one. The mind is one of the most evolved perception mechanisms in our current experience since we can use it to try to comprehend our other senses, thinking about and interpreting them. Nevertheless, it is not the ultimate mechanism of perception enjoyed by the spirit. Consciousness is not only manifest through the intellectual mind, but in all the senses and mechanisms that a being possesses, whether they know it or not, since it is divine, the universal intelligence acting in the Being. The act of consciousness is eternal, leading the spirit to many new possibilities so that it may continue its evolutionary expansion.

Imagine that for many thousands of years, human beings were developing their physical and adaptive characteristics to the planet they inhabited. When survival circumstances became more precarious, they found themselves acquiring a slightly more elaborate power of communication and the beginnings of language. Understanding that signs began to foster understanding among the people with whom they lived, they began to develop these forms of communication, using sounds and representations. Soon, one individual understood that the symbology they used (now called words) was not only for communicating with others, but those signs also spoke as voices in their own head. They were unaware of the meaning behind this occurrence since it was new for everyone. Anyone who perceived them would follow them. When a voice told them to carry out an action or voice an opinion, the individual responded impulsively, regardless of the nature of the attitude. Those beings did not know the origins and influences of what we currently call thought, or know that most thinking does not derive from individuality itself, that the mind is a field that gathers collective information by tuning in. This new, utilitarian mechanism for human beings was still completely unconscious, and this made individuals identify entirely with the voices in their minds, which developed over the course of thousands of years.

Recently, although many of us still possess considerable levels of unconsciousness, complete obedience to the dictates of the mind is no longer common practice. However, despite the appearance of mental filters and other evolutionary benefits, many individuals still exclusively identify with countless mind processes, in complex conditions, forming distorted ideas about themselves. Even so, through the grace of evolution, an opening to the expansion of consciousness has been deepening considerably on a global scale, to the point that humanity may come to learn about the next steps in perfecting their existential vehicles. Just as in the past the intellectual mind innovated human content, other faculties in development are gradually being experimented with. The first good news is transformation at the level of consciousness of the being because, while survival was once at the forefront of human objectives, the door is gradually opening to a new moment in evolution. Which is founded in unity with Life and doused in the excellence of love, on another level of sensitivity and clarity. Before long, having raised our mental qualities, we will all begin participating in a new and comprehensive process of the miracle of life.

The development of the human ego was part of a universal process, and having been accomplished, it is now on the threshold of transcending to support a new form of dealing with the intelligence of the being. This will continue among those who choose it, especially over the course of this and the coming generations. The ego's characteristic of pursuing its own survival above everything else, inherited from animals, is evolving towards an emergence of conscious coexistence, which can only be sustained by love. To this end, we will consider elucidating forms of dealing with the mind, so we may transcend its normal mechanisms and paradigms.

When you have something that you consider a problem to be solved and are at a loss, do not limit yourself to asking your mind a question and waiting for a definitive answer on how to solve it. There might be many answers and alternatives willing to present themselves in order that you choose, meanwhile you are closed and only hearing a single limited response that your mind will choose for you through affinity. It will probably be an answer that the mind already knows, or something close to it. In these cases, the question would also be like a horse wearing blinders, with many answers popping up all around him, and yet he does not see them, because he was wearing the blinders of the question.

There is no single right answer for each and every thing; Life is infinite and accomplished through many possibilities.

When we ask a single question, we demand a single answer. It would be better to let the information come in "blocks." This way, complete sets can flow through an open mind, and millions of answers can emerge, instead of questions that confuse the mind. It is not to say that you should stop asking questions, only do not limit yourself to them. Open yourself flexibly to the most sublime information around you, instead of just spinning around the words and concepts of your intellect. At times, faced with a question, individuals await an answer in the field of words, searching in their mental anxiety. Yet it is in the kingdom of energy and presence that all information dwells. If you find yourself confused when making a decision, do not get caught up in your questions; they will just roam in an attempt to analyze what they do not yet know based on what they already know conceptually. Equally, do not get caught up in the need for answers. Let them flow. Simply allow yourself to let them in.

From an early age, many individuals are trained to see everyday situations as problems (like simple math equations). They then attribute negative emotions to problems and positive ones to solutions. The point is that, generally, over the course of life, the moments of something being solved are extremely short, while the time spent trying to understand and solve problems is long. In this way, individuals are involved in emotions seen as negative a great deal of their time. We only view problems from a negative perspective when we believe them to be negative, based on how we accept them as we identify with them. We can go about our everyday lives just the same without any of them, since what we call a problem is a way of seeing the world, a belief. To this end, we can change our daily lives if we direct our focus towards conscious observation, abandoning the paradigm of negative problems and embracing challenges and experiences as *opportunities* that bring light to the present situation. Circumstances can be graciously transformative when free from views that condemn them as problems tied to negative emotions. A natural sentiment from our interior blossoms when we see them as opportunities. Wherever there is an idea that something is a problem, accompanied by dramatization, we are not truly showing up here and now, since we are caught up in the emotional drama of a personal story. Therefore, instead of setting up an obstacle in the present, it works better to become one with it.

We can be non-judgmental observers, opening ourselves to the best that each moment asks for. If we are mindful, all the information we are open to receiving is available, making the most eminent choice clear for our present moment. A living synchronicity surrounds us, supplying information that goes beyond who we are. Moments of synchronicity happen all the time, everywhere. When they are perceived, we often call them coincidences. However, they are not always acknowledged, except when they are right in front of us. When they go unnoticed, in practice, they are only ignored through non-attention. We are all immersed in living synchronicity. There is nothing that is not a result of universal synergy in perfect harmony with our beliefs and choices.

All choices synchronize with reality. When you choose something in your life, you create the path toward it. At times, this creation lies in giving yourself over to the choice. If you want something different, you will not get it by doing the same thing. Unless you do the same externally, transforming who you are internally. It is not what we do that truly matters, but how we do it.

Human accomplishment is the path, not just an end. In fact, an end is when a series of moments occurring along the path become palpable to unite as an experienceable result. There is only an end contextually because, in essence, the eternal present moment is the final purpose. Therefore, to solve a path, we face it as a true opportunity, liberating it without adding obstacles or barriers to our worldview.

*Certainty in the future is based on everyday acts of faith because the now is all that exists.* To create a future, bring it into your present. Find all the elements of what you are choosing that are already within your grasp and lend your observation to them.

If choosing joy and prosperity, open yourself to joy now and be thankful for everything that is already prosperous in your life. Even the small things. Begin by looking at them frequently in your life, and you will make them multiply. Soon you will be aware of how they reach you and others. It might seem like you are fooling yourself, thinking about how to stay happy now, if it is not yet the case. However, the mind that believes it needs something preempts any other solution by projecting it always into the future, just as the mind that believes in doubt does not want it solved, for doubt only wants more of itself. Instead, surrender yourself to the essence; bring your perception here. Search for what is present within you that you do not see yet, not for something that is not. Do this without expectations, merely enjoying right now whatever is already true of what you are choosing. In this way, you will feel it as part of your reality, making it multiply itself.

If something smells bad, do we just stand there annoyed, next to the foul smell, smelling it? Why do so many of us stubbornly stand by suffering, as if inhaling the air of affliction? We do understand human difficulties; however, choice is always in effect.

We may remain aware that when we clean something, the dirt can return. Enjoy cleanliness while it lasts, but do not condemn the dirt when it comes. Do not try to hold onto the cleanliness, so it will ever end. Simply enjoy it. Taking great mood in your daily health and hygiene routine, in good spirits and willingness, is time better spent than condemning or resisting all forms of dirt. Because beyond "dirty" or "clean," what truly makes a difference in becoming aware are the internal states that you cultivate. Dirt exists, and it will reappear to remind us of its existence. After all, we know it is all our own creation, do we not? In nature, there is no intrinsic pattern of cleanliness; it is only part of our relative creation. In conscious unity with nature, everything becomes clean as a whole. Incidentally, that word is no longer appropriate. All terms aside, everything is naturally as it is.

If we like cleanliness, how can we clean something that is not dirty? How can we know love if we have never known fear? How do we know happiness without experiencing sadness? If we like daytime, can we perceive it without the night? If there is no old, how can we know what is new?

If one side of the coin pleases you, enjoy it and thank the other side for existing; one exists because of the other. In fact, "the coin" of Life does not have two sides, it is only the mind that perceives dualistically. There are more than just two poles, the variables and possibilities are infinite. Life is a coin of many sides. The mind grabs on to a referential, seeing duality from its point of view. Beyond it, there is an infinite and interminable Universe that does not fit into words. Having those two poles of mental experience is not a problem. However, not only do we get used to limiting ourselves, but we also reject and condemn one side of the polarity. As long as there is a single mind still stating that the male sex is the only deserving sex or that the right side is the correct side, we will always be incomplete.

Unity lies in merging the duality and the pluralism of variables to be able to transcend them. May we begin by living duality fully. Although many of us still try to start our day on the right foot, do we not? Why not start on the left? Or both? For all that, those who prefer using only their right foot could become impaired. Impaired in love, insofar as we do not deal with our fear. Impaired in our masculinity, since we are unable to perceive the feminine inside us. Impaired as we face the new, at a loss when struggling to reconcile it with what we classify as old. Impaired on the right, inasmuch as we despise the left. And so forth. So, is it possible to experience each side of duality as one? Yes, it is. Use either your right or your left leg on their own whenever you like, but most likely you will end up using both to walk, united in synergy.

The Universe is pure acceptance, because if there were something that it truly did not accept, this something could not possibly exist. Curiously, the Universe accepts all possibilities, since after all, it is infinite possibilities. Therefore, it accepts itself, seeing that it is everything. In the same way, we can sense that whenever we condemn something, we deny ourselves. Both in terms of what is inside and outside of us. After all, inside and outside are two poles, and if we deny one, we will be denying ourselves. What would happen to you internally if there were no you externally? How could you know about one without the other? Considering that united, there is only one.

Thus, we are each both observer and observed participant, one does not exist without the other. Observe yourself observing yourself.

Observe how the mind does not contain the Being since it is infinite. You participate in what you call reality. Then you observe yourself participating in it. Still later, you observe yourself observing yourself. Following that sequence, who is the one who observes you watching you observe? Effectively, spirit and consciousness are the origin and source of every observation, on a multiplicity of levels. Therefore, everything that observes and is observed flows in consciousness, in a universal field of energy.

The mind is like a camera, recording mental images that freeze moments on the screen of perception. When not taking pictures, it opens past photo albums, viewing its many records, at times creating collages with the available images, editing possible futures. Nonetheless, perception beyond the mind is not sustained by loose pieces of isolated figures, but through awareness of a constant and malleable flow. We can liken it to a movie where the subject is, simultaneously, spectator (observer), protagonist (participant) and director (creator), flowing while it moves in the eternal present.

A well-balanced mind allows the being's *genuine desire* to emerge, which does not come from the mind, but it merely passes through it. Coming from the essence, the choice originates in the will of the spirit; consequently, it illumines and enlightens the mind, which opens itself to feel the meaning beyond the words. It forms a bridge that starts with genuine willingness, and its intention flows through the open mind, manifesting it into action.

If the mind is confused and restricted to untamed thoughts, the paths are different. Among them, a confused ego obfuscates the inner-space, since it is in disharmony with the being and in conflict with what it received from the exterior world. In this case, authentic intention seeks a place to enter, but there is none. The mind is not open, present and attentive, but disarranged by all the thoughts about itself and the world. The more we fill our mind with incessant thoughts, the more veiled the essence becomes. Having blocked the path that allows the choice of a clear will, the feeling of confusion increases, while the field of desires becomes a "no man's land", and broadly suggestible.

Considering that the being's true will has been obfuscated and no longer finds any more room to flow, as an alternative, the ego replaces it with another intention, one we will call *false will*. It is based on thoughts originating predominantly from the exterior. In other words, the individual's will becomes, in part, the will of the surrounding world. Under these terms, many of us unconsciously take on social roles in nearly all our relationships, as a result of an imbalanced connection between ego and true will.

Since this will is false, it is not self-supporting. Only the legitimate intention emerges and is nourished by the innermost Being. As a result, the false desire needs to be fed. It has to make an effort to feed itself. It has to lend great importance to the choices based on the apparent want. Energy is its nourishment. This is how disputes and imagery games arise, since the need for energy leads it to fight for power, attacking and defending in an exacerbated attempt to stay alive, even in the most minimal and subtle relationships within its reach. It is likely that the ego struggles with other false wills to keep its wheel spinning. In this case, we come to want more of what others want, something the external world demands of us. You can see how individuals strongly believe that those desires are originally their own, that they are part of their identity, when in fact they were accepted as such.

This has notably been occurring at all social levels, still considered by the majority as levels in relationship to external power. What we call social classes are still classified according to purchasing power, by what we have, not who we are. Material goods and acquisitions can be useful, but do we want to measure ourselves by them? In some societies considered primitive, people valued themselves for who they were and who they chose to be, not for what they had. Those who led them were beings of wisdom within that context. There were jobs for women, men, and space for children; no one was greater or lesser. They were all integral parts of a large web. Although they recognized individuals by who they chose to be and honored these differences, they understood uniqueness and respected each person's path as part of the whole.

In some indigenous civilizations, and not only in them, participants were not regarded by classes, but as integral parts of a larger group. There were shamans, seamstresses, warriors, fishers, toolmakers, sowers, harvesters, chiefs, counselors, hunters, intertribal messengers, midwives, and artists, among others. What is more, societies such as these saw each job as belonging to a single circle. Symbolically, each being in the group was holding hands with those around them to form a circle. Nobody deserved more or less, they were only brothers and sisters performing complementary jobs.

Symbolically, many beings in our current society still think of themselves as standing in some sort of line. Those at the front of the line are considered the first and best, while those at the end are considered the last and worst. Such inequality easily leads some to resolve to break the line. In contrast, the characteristic of essential will is for everyone to win, to be empowered along with everyone else. When a false will loses (everyone loses sometimes since they are in constant battle), there is frustration. In other words, deep down they are always, whether deeply or superficially, marked by fear. However, as long as there is competition for survival, some false wills will always come out losing, while others win; until we realize that everyone loses that way. True will is always related to love, and when there is love, there are no battles to wage since life need not be tolerated as an act of survival, but lived in a way that it is appreciated and celebrated. Happy are those who share in the unity of the circle, so that, through evolution, they may expand its circumference, achieving greater reach.

There's nothing wrong or right in corresponding to the false will since right and wrong are relative — they depend on a referential. Nonetheless, we are surely making choices all the time and finding its results. It is an experience, both individual and collective. Often, it becomes indispensable for the person to experience illusory wills as much as they believe it necessary. The results serve as opportunities for awakening until moments of natural desire expand themselves. At times, as far as an individual is unconscious, the spirit's deepest will patiently honor the beliefs that formulate false wills, making this kind of experience possible until consciousness transforms the being's choices. This edifying process shows us the way in which the Spirit and Life honor the nature of all choices. The fleeting existence of illusory desires can serve as comprehensive material for the individual, initiating clarification before the genuine will.

The state of *depression* is directly tied to the relationship between true and false will. Depression's prime characteristic is the internal state of paralysis, though the body may still move and the routine may still be the same. In this state, both false and authentic will are blocked, and the person experiences an absence of motive. The energy of depression is like standing water. Energy that flows and runs freely is incessantly renewed on its way to its natural state. Will is what makes the "water" mobilize itself, generating more energy as it lives.

If the mind were a river, depression would be the dam, stopping the water. What raises the dam is the inner conflict between false and true will, which is reflected in the vision about life. After bearing the heavy load of illusory desires in everyday living, the individual wears out and intuitively "drains" the need to cultivate them, while also forgetting its own essentiality, at least in some respects. Exhausted and believing it has no other option, it blocks the only one it thought it knew, temporarily annulling itself in a stagnation of movement. Feeling no reason to live, the individual believes there is no other way out and is paralyzed, like stagnant water.

Through these periods of transformation humanity is experiencing, we are increasingly seeing people showing signs of depression, while others become even more intensely entrenched in that condition. In the former, the dam is partial and depression *initial*. At times, it comes and goes. In the latter, the dam prevents any water from passing through, and depression is *established*. Depression is not superficial, on the contrary. It is a deeply transformational experience of the being, allowing them to abandon some of the mental hang-ups and go deep within the misunderstanding of themselves. It is common for people to enter into conflict with God at that point, as if life no longer had any meaning, given that they do not comprehend what is happening to them in their inner spheres, which is part of the process. Nevertheless, an internal and external healing and harmonization can result from a deep and fulfilling closeness with the essence, which always makes self-renewal possible. As soon as the world views depression from this perspective, society will be transformed, dissipating ephemeral social pressures and desires, and allowing humanity's innermost nature to come forth with its most illustrious intentions.

There is also the case where the individual, instead of blocking off the false will, can unconsciously exaggerate it, remaining completely in full identification with it. In this predisposition towards pain, imbalanced mental structures are created, setting off processes and manias that tend towards *insanity*. If the mind were a lake, mental insanity would be the appearance of pollution in its waters, making it unhealthy. Pollution arises from noxious thoughts that are absorbed and cultivated, leading the individual to madness in the absence of their natural mental clarity.

Among other states, madness is a result of the accumulation of unresolved, unharmonized internal processes. Observing society's current condition, we see countless people cultivating different levels of insanity. Some are considered socially acceptable, in small personal, familiar and social conflicts, while others are not so well accepted, in disorders that standout from the everyday established rules. Note that we are not considering madness as a process discordant with patterns of social normality, but as a disturbance in individuals dealing with internal aspects which conflict with their own conscience and ability to maintain some balance. None of these occurrences constitute who the person truly is, only how they are at that moment.

To mention these topics is relevant since, during this moment in time experienced by humanity, in parallel with the transformation of a new world, countless individuals find themselves with immense internal and external difficulties, from depression to mental insanity. We are not here to judge any of those cases, but to provide support and understanding that we might find what lies beyond the beliefs that created such realities. For those who are wide awake, our suggestion is neither condemn nor resist your life companions; just be the support the world needs through love and by setting an example. Before long, we will increasingly build bonds of unity to aid current conditions, consolidating renewal of the human experience.

There is innate beauty in human beings truly and humbly opening themselves to be helped, along with someone who can help, united in a transformative purpose. When two or more people come together in sincere, joint intention, marvelous things arise. Nevertheless, considering life in general, sometimes people will appear along the existential journey who, although they suffer and feel bad, are so attached to their *way of life* that they do not want direct assistance. At those times, respect and compassion are the best approaches. At times, it is good to simply open the window and let the other person to nurture the desire to look outside.

For those who are open to it, genuine assistance stirs up the movement of the inner will. One individual's light temporarily kindles the light in another, making new forces of true expression possible. It is like someone who carefully nudges their younger sibling along on their bicycle, so they can start pedaling on their own. If they do not know how to nudge them correctly and are too rough because of their false will, the sibling might end up falling off the bicycle, and depending on the circumstances might not want to try again. Still, when successful, prepared through love, they can joyfully pedal along the highways of life.

All true assistance spontaneously flows through what it is, in beautiful and deep relationships among spirits, encouraging standing water to pour naturally. In that case, may unconditional love be the star that guides human intention.

Plants and trees are perhaps the beings closest to unconditional love on the material level. Unconditional love is to human beings, as trees, in nature, are to the living beings around them. They love silently and at times go unnoticed, providing constant peace to the environment, regardless of who notices them. They do not force anyone to do anything, but instead, they offer serenity and well-being to all those present. They do not hold back from or offend anyone; they simply supply oxygen so that others may breathe. They do not become attached to their visitors, and they offer themselves up through their branches, leaves and fruits, which become food and fertilizer for other beings. They do not impose anything on anyone; they only encourage inspiration and quietude in whomever it may be, through their presence. Like love, trees create paths for our journey, never interfering in our freedom, only gently encouraging it.

# CHAPTER 12

The ego is one of today's most talked-about subjects. It is currently considered a new villain, alongside many others who have made or still are part of our history. Maybe we can take this opportunity to end the myth of the villain in humanity. First, in a simple manner, we will take another look at what is considered to be the ego.

Originally, the term meant "I" and was used in the same way that we currently use the first person singular, but in Latin. The meaning attributed to the expression has now gone beyond this use, having changed throughout history. The expression is now used as the individual's conception of their own personality — the idea or representation of their self, mostly formed through its relationship with the outside environment. The ego develops mental and emotional structures about itself in this world. From this perspective, the ego is a space that lies between you as an individual and the outside world. Clearly, it is not your skin, but a structured environment created between the outer and inner space. It is a composition that arises in the mind to absorb and use the information provided by the external world. From the moment of your birth, people have described their perceptions of the world to you, and the ego absorbed all the content with which you agreed from the surrounding environment, which tends to occur easily because a growing child is very open.

The ego manifests itself through a few fundamental structures. Since it is composed of mental information, memory is one of the ego's foundation blocks. This creates an automatic link with a notion of time, which stirs up mental reactions, not just from memories of the past, but from their reuse in future projections. This set of memories and projections gives the ego a key role regarding everyday choices that lead to everyday results, making all this information not solely mental, but it also has an intense emotional impact as well. Along the way, the ego becomes shaped by a *time*-based mental/emotional structure, usually coordinated by a social pacemaker. Shaped by the incidence and influence of the surrounding environment, it consequently becomes linked to the *relationship* phenomenon. This is another of its foundation blocks. Wherever there is some form of relationship, the ego will be there. Another of its foundation blocks is brought into existence by the previous ones, through coexistence; the ego creates a *self-image*, a personality with a sense of self, striving to represent the being itself. Finally, an *interpretation* structure appears, from which speculations about reality emerge.

The ego is the reason you walk without stumbling, use fire without burning yourself, read and write without having to relearn everything each time, and are able to talk and relate to others, to name a few of its implications. The ego's fundamental makeup as a mental/emotional structure based on time, relationship, self-image and interpretation is not limited to the ordinary ways those structures have been organized. It not necessary or mandatory to hold on to imbalanced memories, projections and sentiments, a limited and disjointed notion of time, tumultuous relationships, conflicting or insane (to some degree) self-images, and interpretations that are separatist or out of harmony with the natural environment.

Those who began studying the human mind have been very successful in detecting and analyzing each person's ego. A clear recognition of an unconscious ego's antics is the foothold for its transformation. Nevertheless, it has been considered both a villain and a huge obstacle for each of us. For many, life has been about waging war on their own ego. While this is one possible path, it is usually a more painful one.

We can understand these roots well by examining some points in human history. In ancient times, the scant repertoire of ways to share information meant that many messages, metaphors and symbolisms were used to explain the fundamental principles of life and to clarify beliefs, but in many cases, they were also altered. For millennia, parables and metaphors were taught and disseminated over generations, but those who were fearful or powerful either hid or distorted their primordial meaning. On the one hand, we have the essence of these ancient messages as they were originally told, while on the other, we have the interpretations others have given them over time — at times diluting their true nature, and at others distorting it. So, what better way to reach and influence people than with the stories that revolve around their beliefs?

Consequently, those who wanted to have "power" over others, took advantage of symbolisms such as the ones in stories about heaven and hell, and perverted their original meaning. They embedded pre-established ideas, such as the idea that one could never escape from those two destinies, using frightening stories. As those ideas and many others were institutionalized, they created bonds of fear and power. Many saw no other option than to accept these conditions to avoid hell, becoming dependent on the institutions that told them stories that only served their interests. In heaven there were angels, beings of light and perfection that would always help; nevertheless, they would say that only representatives of religious institutions had contact with and access to those beings. The most curious part is how, amid all those concepts, God was supposed to have created everything as a judge who would punish the disobedient, even those who had no knowledge of his law, while at the same time giving them free will. After all, was God worse than the Angels!?

In addition to fearing their own God, personified as a man (intentionally male), who ruled over us as a dictator from his seat in heaven, they also created the character of a devil to frighten people once and for all. This devil ruled hell, where most people would supposedly go after disobeying the power of one who was, contradictorily, omnipotent. Very few would go to heaven, the only place where God in his limitation remained, only those who did not question and followed institutional instructions would be allowed. Many believed them, which is understandable since they were taught this view from birth. At the same time, society and politics were both organized around it. However, there have always been those who found and lived the essence of the messages.

Since their beginnings, humans have been able to observe the principles of life, whatever they could perceive in that moment. They noticed the forces that made life flow, and created representations of them. Still, those who did not comprehend the enigmas of spiritual stories, personified God and the devil as two males fighting each other since they were only self-likenesses unconsciously projected. For their own self-interest, there were situations in which the characteristics and content of the stories that were told were purposely altered and selected to have an effect on people. Many ancient words saw their original meanings twisted so that the emerging religious institution could preclude others from using the same expressions.

Ancient expressions did not have the same meaning we attribute them today. The meaning given to expressions can change over time. For example, the term devil arose from the Greek civilization, derived from the word *diabolos*, which means to divide, to separate. The word demon derives from the Latin *daemon* and the Greek *daimon*, meaning spirit, genie, divinity or spirit guide. The term Satan arose from the Latin *satana*, from the Greek *satanas*, from the Hebrew *satan*, meaning adversary. Those and other expressions were distorted for millennia while they took divergent paths. Ancient spiritualists who came before the emergence of religious institutions and usually not associated with them used the word devil to express the idea of separation from God. The word demon spoke of the spirits who interacted with everyone; it did not necessarily have a good or bad connotation. They used the word Satan to demonstrate the appearance of an adversarial impulse, the existence of individual and collective negativity, an opposing impulse from the unconscious human who denies life, either in themselves or the surrounding world.

Still, other individuals have personified the devil as something awful and fearful. So they went from something to someone who would have such characteristics. The same condemnation with the word demon, so no one would be able to contact spirits outside religious institutions. The same was done with the word satan, portraying all three as a malefic entity, vulgarly portrayed as red and horned, associating it with images and adulterating the meaning of many illustrious messages regarding energetic principles. The fact is that the same could have been done to any other word. Thus, some religious and political institutions distracted people's attention away from spiritualists and their true intentions, which lead to profound changes. They modified these and other terms, so they could monopolize common beliefs. For this reason, many wars have been waged throughout history, promoted by those who fooled themselves, claiming to carry out massacres in the name of spiritualists or God.

The age-old purpose of churches is not to blame. Even amid much confusion, they have spread part of the message's little understood structure over the centuries. Rather, it is the responsibility of those within the churches who changed their course, even though there are those who have left behind truly beneficial contributions. After all, unbalanced human beings tend to do anything in order to wield power over others who lack power over themselves. Religions owe it to themselves to take another look at the essence of the stories they have taken upon themselves to promote, which are so rich in origin. Actually, if we look deep, this is a responsibility of us all.

Since in ancient times, ego and many other words did not exist ot did not contain their current meanings (for they have also changed over time), those spiritualists strived to use the best that they had to communicate in that context. Another example, regarding word usage over time, is the use of the term reincarnation, which has recently emerged, although its meaning has been understood by all peoples in all corners of the world since the dawn of humanity. Previously, other words and ways were used to broach the subject, such as the idea of the soul transmigrating to other bodies, rebirth, treated for millennia as metempsychosis. Parables have also been used as a way for teachings to continue over time, preserving the meaning of the story. However, their meaning was easily distorted and modified. There was no way they could control what each person would do in the continuity of their allegories. However, they knew that truth cannot be defeated. It constantly surrounds us, until it gradually reveals itself. In light of this, reading ancient scriptures only through time-altered concepts is the same as not truly understanding them, but if you look for the essence of their message, you will decipher them.

By way of comparison, the words satan and devil have both been used in varying situations with a meaning similar to the one recently attributed to ego, be it individually or collectively. Some spiritualists have suggested that we overcome the adversary within us, and transcend the influences from the outer world that we have received since birth by connecting to the kingdom of heaven. Imagine if centuries from now the term ego became distorted, wrapped in fear and darkness, and associated with images and artistic paintings. It makes it possible for us to understand what happened to other words throughout history, especially those with allegorical content.

Heaven and hell were equal participants in a grand story about positive and negative principles in the human experience, composed of enigmas illustrating the nature of energy amid life, not merely external places intended to hold them forever. As one of those spiritualists, Jesus stated this same principle when he said: "The kingdom of God cometh not with outward show. Neither shall they say: Lo here! or Lo there! For, behold, the kingdom of God is within you." – 21st Century King James Version (KJ21) – Luke 17:20-21.

It is easy to see how much society tends to infuse dread in its concepts. Society habitually repeats this feat in its myths, stories, drawings, movies, and advertising. Industry frequently uses this in the same way some religious institutions have, to manage people's fears, based on market demands, in order to sell their products. Fear is the bait, power is the hook.

The same has been done, on another scale, regarding the ego, which can be your adversary, if you so choose. You are free to spend your life fighting it if you like. The ego's existence is no mistake; it is only that numerous difficulties are created when it remains in a state of disequilibrium. These conflicts are understandable, having been taught this way for generations. After all, with so many villains outside, why would there not be one inside as well? If so many people fight, is it not normal to fight with oneself? Those questions are likely, considering society's established creations. Still, we can choose to maintain the cycle or create another, a better one.

There might be, in fact, a negative characteristic in human beings, which could be called darkness. The ego can often harbor such forces, but only when its field gives in to carelessness and instability. That is not the nature of the ego, only a temporary condition that many people and society adopt, to a greater or lesser extent. Negative existence was created precisely to give the light a way to manifest itself since its job is to illuminate the darkness, within and without.

If an individual is not aware of what originates from within or without, it will cause one to interfere in the naturalness of the other, generating imbalance. Clarity of spirit is lacking, which affords a clear view of the ego, the spirit's instrument. Thanks to the ego, you are reading this book right now, as much as thanks to the eyes. Thanks to the ego, you can have relationships with others. This is not a burden, but a blessing! Unless you would rather see it as a burden.

Fundamentally, a human being's mind consists of three spaces. The first is similar to a field ready for sowing — the ego. The second is the earth beneath the field, nourished by nutrients or pollutants — the channel of the mind, which is receptive to the outer world and supplies itself with information. The third is the sky above the soil — the intuitive mind, or channel of inspiration, which illuminates it with sunbeams and irrigates the earth with rain, comprising all the previous conditions. When this relationship is complete, the field is ready for a beneficial harvest. However, when the soil obtains few nutrients, making it barren, or when it receives all kinds of artificial pollutants, depending on which concepts the ego embraces, this prevents light and water from penetrating it cleanly.

In one of these three channels is where intuition, inspiration and insight occur, where essential information of the being flows, linked to its true will. We can call this the *inspiration channel*. This is the path for the spirit to communicate with its own mind, and also where spiritual mentors and ally beings tend to relate to individuals, acting through the most essential elements of their being.

Another channel is where external information enters your mind, receiving whatever other people and the world have been feeding you over time. We can call it the *external-receptive channel*. Many began debasing the ego because it frequently, although not always, shapes itself after the extraneous dissonance coming from this channel. In addition, when inner aspects exist in a state of confusion, it is usually through this entryway, since it is possible for disincarnate beings who are also in a state of conflict to come near and have some type of energetic influence, just like incarnate beings have on their relationships. For this reason, although spiritual influences exist, one of the keys to healing lies in contemplating one's own internal channels through the being's conscientiousness.

The third, a central space in the mental field, is the *ego*. This is the field where information coming from the outside is stored and used, as well as information coming from within. As if this space lay between the other two channels. Therefore, if well used, the ego is a tool that creates balance between the inner and outer spaces, a connection between the formless and form. Effectively, we might say that the other two channels are like bridges or entryways into the mind, while the ego is the space that receives and unites them.

Actually, if we take a good look at several of its main characteristics, it would be more precise to give the ego another name; with a tinge of humor, we could call it the *echo*. That simple word says a lot about this instrument's nature, which resonates in the mind what the senses pick up day after day. As the ego receives external and internal information, it resonates this information internally, echoing it in the mind before responding in what can be called *return*. The ego correlates essential information from the being's center that flows through the inspiration channel with information from the external-receptive channel, generating a harmonious or imbalanced return. In practice, the ego does nothing alone, it just responds as programmed according to the flow of energy that runs through it. When balanced, the being's inspiration flows through the ego, illuminating each piece of information it receives, using it to bring light to the world.

There is no reason to destroy the ego. That would just be an attempt to extinguish a part of yourself, amid resistance and internal conflict. There is no need to turn it into a villain. However, when predominantly composed by disagreeing influences, and less by the being's essence, its tendency is to create a "separate I," generating illusions and suffering. Hardship has never been part of the ego itself, but of its discordant constitution; therefore, a well-balanced ego is the conception of a "united I." By renouncing the "separate I" and seeing himself as Life itself, Jesus demonstrated this feat in a variety of actions and statements, such as, "I am the way, the truth, and the life." – King James Bible – John 14:6.

His goal was not to be the only one in that condition, as if it were impossible for everyone else, but to invite those who listened to him to learn about this complete and natural state of being, making sacred communion with the divine our purpose. So, when he discusses the themes in the Sermon on the Mount, he said to everyone: "Be ye therefore perfect, even as your Father which is in heaven is perfect." – King James Bible – Matthew 5:48. His purpose was not to announce that he was the only one capable of such feats, exclusively as Jesus, but to show us we can transcend the "separate I" as we connect ourselves to the "united I," by doing it himself. His statement was radiant when he said: "The words that I speak unto you I speak not of myself: but the Father that dwelleth in me, he doeth the works." – King James Bible – John 14:10. Soon after, he adds: "Verily, verily, I say unto you, He that believeth on me, the works that I do shall he do also; and greater works than these shall he do." – King James Bible – John 14:12.

Like all spiritual masters, Jesus also had an ego— like anyone else experiencing the human condition, with the profound difference that those who have penetrated this mastery transcend barriers and realign their "I" with Life itself, rather than maintaining an "I" excluded from the rest. To confirm this, he clearly and openly stated to everyone, "I and the Father are one."

The imbalanced ego latches onto resistance. Everything you resist, re-exists. Natural fluency is disallowed amid excessive and disconnected thoughts. Notwithstanding, a balanced ego is permeated with surrender to the experience of the eternal present moment. In that state, there are energies indescribable to concepts and an absence of judgment, preoccupation, resistance, or reaction to the world. Only your unmitigated observance and unlimited space to create here and now, expressing your loving and conscious presence. Leaving the vicious cycle of reacting, like someone fighting their own tail, you begin to act on the essential. Surrendering yourself to spirit and no longer identifying with a "separate I" opens a channel in your being so that natural consciousness can flow through you, while spontaneously bringing balance to your mental instruments.

If you have been receiving information from the world since birth that has hindered your relationship with your intuition and true will, this will be somewhat of a shock to your ego. What came from the outside, through your external receptive mind, served as material to create structures that block what comes from within. When one of them crops up, it fogs your relationship with your intuitive mind. This clash with your true will, or its absence, generates a series of reactions that leave your ego in disagreement, and it begins to send an unharmonious response to the world.

In this case, this can lead to disorientation, because you are unable to fully accept what the external world conveys to you, just as you may not be successfully discerning everything your intuition wants to present to you. The three spaces begin to disagree, and you end up not having a clear awareness of the aspects related to the blocking of these channels. If the way you express your sexuality is imbalanced in some way, for example, internal and external information will begin to collapse, in such a way that your ego will no longer have the structure and stability to properly deal with sexual experiences. You will feel that confusion internally, as well as in your practical life, where it will manifest itself tumultuously. When you modify the external patterns received, which causes your sexuality to become somewhat unbalanced (as per the example above), in such a way that the ego becomes translucent and cleans your relationship with the external-receptive channel, you will no longer burden it with that dissonant information. Soon, there will be room for your intuitive mind to begin communicating clearly how to express your sexuality sublimely, starting from yourself, allowing you to balance your ego and make your sexual experience sacred. When your mental and emotional spaces are harmonized and fully processed, a sensation of natural flow takes over your being in relation to the aspects found within.

We are multidimensional beings, so several aspects in each of us are in processes of imbalance or balance. It would be imprecise to divide people into categories of entirely balanced or imbalanced because every individual has multiple unknown areas that act in their existence and are part of their own movements. Each individual is in their moment of what we call evolution. May we have the humility to acknowledge our own experience.

The ego is part of your experience of the world. However, when considering reincarnation, we see that there are highly refined and detailed structures of the mind restricted to a particular existence. There are other deeper structures, like foundations of your mental functioning and way of thinking, which continue on as tendencies from one lifetime to another, exerting influence unless they are transformed. Hence, the ego is the represented "I," or better said, part of the manifestation of the "I." However, the essential I, core of the being, much more than the thoughts wandering and ephemeral emotions, is consciousness itself that observes, chooses and is a spectator of itself.

The ego is an excellent element for self-observation since it echoes your experiences. Through attention and contemplation, we see that it is always showing us what experience is providing us. Because it generates feedback, it is something by which we determine our experience in the world. Thus, when flowing freely through the ego and being present, your consciousness will always demonstrate what the moment is providing so that you can get to know life better. Self-observation is the best way to find yourself because, when you observe yourself, you align with natural consciousness and make healing possible, or at least, a better experience of the spirit's moment.

Clearly comprehending that the ego is one of the being's means of manifestation allows us to understand that identifying with its content is not exactly harmful if aligned with the flow of Life and the spirit. Identifying with the external, restrictive and unconscious factors that the ego received socially, especially in a world permeated with conflict, can bring complications and suffering to anyone. A mind that harbors unhealthy and unnecessary ideas, causing its sense of "I" to identify with them, limits and conditions its being amid illusions, without noticing them. To this end, considering current human conditions, it is more beneficial for us to not identify ourselves so much with the ego's existent mechanisms, such as the usual thoughts and emotions, thus, making it easier for us to anchor our being in the observation of consciousness in a favorable manner. It is like stepping out of a game toward the bleachers and start watching the sports match happening in a stadium from an aerial perspective. In fact, what occurs is an expansion of the identification process, and going from something limited and exclusive to Life as a whole. Upon the success of your goal, and as consciousness continues healing and harmonizing the experience, the being sees the ego reflect the nature of the soul, opening it beneficently to those aspects in conformity with the Universe, in the same way Jesus saw himself as Life itself. In that state, there are no barriers to limit the ego, then the All passes through the ego, and the ego is in the All. The separate ego can see the I as an enemy, whereas the essential I sees the ego as a friendly instrument, transforming the two into one.

Just as your legs serve to walk, the ego serves as your instrument. Would you let your legs go off walking by themselves and, without you being aware, choose where to take your own body? Similarly, would you let your ego be the master of your choices, so they would be unconscious and made directly by the exterior world? Your legs are what make you walk, but something inside you directs them. Your ego provides you a field of experiences, but it is your spirit that includes your entire living being, from where your free will emerges.

The source of your choices can become your expansive self, spirit, which surrounds you as a whole, choosing the most sublime aspects of your will. In this way, your spirit uses the ego as a center for you to experiment in this world. It is similar to a downtown, with so many separate neighborhoods connected to it, carrying goods, supplies and urban services in and out of the central region, just as everything that enters, leaves and is grown, lives in the mind. The harmony of the city as a whole is like spirit in consonance with the mind.

Your body and ego are ways for you to express yourself vehemently. It is inevitable that we receive information assimilated by the ego after we are born. However, what we do with these influences is up to us. Living also consists of absorbing what we choose as necessary, so we can relate with the world or transform it. The mental content known as thoughts or ideas has for the most part been formed by all the information that we accepted before and after birth, always influenced in a variety of ways. Much of what moves about in our mind is not native to our individuality. For example, your entire mother tongue was taught by people around you. Some thoughts arise like a song you hear that gets stuck in your head, echoing. Yet, there are no influences disallowed by the spirit. Not one butterfly lands, not a single hair on your head falls without your being's consent.

Happy are those who in their minds have a fertile field beneficial to all. The ego is like a disciple who waits for their master (spiritual consciousness) to come and outline the tasks, before getting to work and exercising their blessed job amidst other workers. That kind of work is not a burden; it is a blessing.

Only by observing your thoughts attentively, without restrictive identification, does the mold that formed around what you used to believe as your "I" disengages itself, as a mental process that opens this limitless field, in extraordinary resplendent presence. In this way, it understands that all the signs of life around it are in consonance with the Living Spirit. At times, that state of self-contemplation not only provides you with the most sublime sentiments, it naturally shows you those ancient aspects that exist hidden in your mind, so you can observe and work with them, expanding your consciousness. The land of the ego becomes enlightened, since it is not light itself, but an instrument used to reveal it. Like the moon reflects sunlight, the ego can reflect the light of the being.

# CHAPTER 13

A long the twists and turns of the human mind, *needy mental forms* are habitually created. When a need exists and manifests itself, it does not constitute who you really are, but seeks nourishment from your thoughts, emotions, and attitudes, while also inciting reactions in others. Your being does not have specific needs: it is only what you are doing in a certain context in your life that needs something to continue being done. However, when the being precedes the doing, the two become one. Most people believe they have needs they otherwise would not have if they did not believe in them, because they have been learned and can be modified. When those needs stop hijacking our thoughts and decisions, an inner space of surrender, acceptance and awareness of the living state opens.

There is a vast diversity of needs with which many people tend to identify. We see the consequences most openly in addiction, burning desire for sex, drugs, food, digital devices, and more stereotypical habits and customs; however, they occur intensely in the subtlety of every day thoughts, where their systems are established. As each one begins, a space in the mind is marked and set up, creating a mental formation that develops its own will. Which needs do you believe you have?

Every need has a beginning. Every moment characterized by unconsciousness where marks have been left, both within the family or outside it, create a structure that responds to the event in a child's mind and emotions. That structure tends to be based on a need that creates a mental form.

Here is a specific example. Someone who felt a lack of familial love in their childhood might create a subtle need and will strive to fill it in current situations through other types of relationships, customarily with their spouse, or at other times just in their own mental fantasies. The most interesting part, however contradictory, lies in observing how, within the workings of the mind, the real objective of any needy mental form is not to achieve a permanent solution to the "problem." The deeper purpose is always to find themselves just as needy as before, or even more so. The mental form seeks a supply of energy, in other words, a self-repeating need.

Someone who feels a lack will search for something to fill this void. Nevertheless, individuals are usually ignorant of the mental form's true objective, not knowing how the structure works. Rather, the thoughts originating from it constantly lead them back to repeating needs, keeping the form active and in control. When a matrimonial relationship tries to occupy this space – sometimes confused with a distorted idea of "love," before long that person will become discontent, and expect their companion to supply the feeling, demanding and pressuring for behavior the other is not willing to give. Whether they succeed or not, little by little they will move on to the next stage, desiring a relationship with someone else, even if only in their minds. The manner in which the needs are expressed may change from relationship to relationship, but at the core they remain the same, to nourish the needy mental form. This is why, when a need appears, individuals believe they can end it by fulfilling their desire. However, when they finally do, what in fact occurs is temporary satisfaction that soon reverts to dissatisfaction. It is another entry in the ledger that strengthens the field of need.

Even if you consider your needs to be beneficial, the fact that you continually need them to happen to you demonstrates the amount of time, attention and energy employed, when, instead, it could be spent in the benefit of many. You only have to make the choice. When spiritual presence arises as a cultivated attribute, every activity can be carried out willingly, joyfully, wholly, and spontaneously. Instead of frequently feeling a lack in any given situation, simply cultivate that moment in yourself through its occurrences.

Mental forms need to grow in size and energy; this is the fire that feeds them. In many cases, we call this addiction. Nonetheless, it is a good idea to remain aware that, when there is addiction, it is not our being that is in fact addicted; rather it is the mental form dwelling within us that demands whatever will allow it to survive. Ceasing to feed a mental form will cause it to let go of the energy it has monopolized for so long. At first, the form will demand what it needs and has been taken away, but before long, its structures will begin to dissolve, freeing up that energy once again, making it available for new creations.

There are cases known as attachments not traditionally considered addictions. An attachment is a needy mental form seeking for what it feels it needs. When there is obvious attachment, the nature of that feeling does not come from your essential being, but from a mental form that developed that need. As you dismantle the attachment barrier, dissolving it in freedom, a clear space opens for the spirit's intrinsic feeling to emerge.

Sooner or later, desire becomes harmful when the attachment to what we want becomes an irrevocable need, thereby creating a connection of dependency. When the origin of desire is limited to the mental field, if we observe it attentively, we will see that this yearning would rather not see an end. As soon as it is fulfilled, it immediately seeks for the next occasion to ensure its survival. Fleeting as it is, the need cries out to continue its existence.

On the other hand, a desire of the spirit is constant and free from any oscillation, accompanied as it is by the peace of its genuineness, free of any need. One of the principles of knowing oneself is to recognize the sincere intention always available to your being. When desire aligns itself with the spirit's genuine will, it vibrates naturally and intensely, equivalent to an open flow. In one case, desire is what dominates the individual, while in the other, the individual is the one who takes advantage of the more eminent desire, interlaced with the wisdom of the spirit.

The soul does not have any needs, for it is resplendent in the fullness and immanence of the being. The soul does not need anything.

However, amid the manifestations, needs arise, in the field where body and mind live and cultivate the feeling that they lack something that completes them. All needs acquired by the body and mind are transitory, since both are ephemeral. Those who seek the living truth will always find it, regardless of their needs, since it is in the living source where consciousness and soul are united in the present moment. As far as transitory mechanisms of the body and mind are drawn into this juncture, the needs demanded begin to fade away, one by one. Meanwhile, by transcending temporary needs, we make room for the spirit to act, amid goals aligned with the natural flow of the living moment.

In fact, many circumstances have needs that need to be met. There are certain professions that incite the need of preparing the individual to receive a diploma. However, your Being does not need a diploma. It is the profession that requires those qualifications. Another example we see every day is food, since hunger implores you to meet its needs. Still again, your spirit does not need the food, it is a condition of your body, which serves you as an instrument. All transitory structures tend to need something; to the spirit, they all appear to be opportunities. Observing these examples, we can note how circumstances and their relative contexts can demand needs. However, since they are all temporary to their situations, not identifying with them as if they constituted your own "I" is an open door to freedom!

Wisdom gives each person the ability to comprehend current circumstances as many possibilities for choice, not as needs to be met. As belief in human needs fades, there are no more attachments, addictions, or irrevocable demands. All situations become fitting occasions amid universal life, leading to a change in our worldview. Fortunate are those not taken over by their needs, but who live each moment as it is in contentment, nourishing the vastness existing in the now, through the opportunity to choose to anchor the spirit in the daily actions.

The fundamental question of this possibility is not whether we should change our relationships or our daily tasks and activities. Foremost, it is about raising awareness of our inner space and perhaps find out what muddled it. It is no longer about needing a pious agreement with the mental programming. When clear observation leads to awareness of the needy forms that have become established in your mind, the first attitude you have is to recognize them without resistance or self-judgment. You accept their existence and then transform them through the light of your spirit.

As you undergo these healing processes, if on occasion you find yourself anxious, confused, nervous or having trouble dealing with your mind and its emotions, trying to understand questions you have about yourself, your life, or decisions to make, remember that is not the time to make decisions. It is time to accept that there is nothing you need to do or define for the time being. If the needs that you believe you have are protesting and arising, from the moment the greater desire for transformation emerges in your being, you no longer identify with those same ones that used to control you. In some cases, part of the liberation process can mean those established marks will complain – at times mercilessly. Recognizing that, at the time, you are not in your full and whole state and accepting the situation as it is, will be beneficial to you. As soon as you stop worrying about the results of something to be solved and begin contemplating your own presence, whatever must come will naturally enter your awareness. Allow the essence of your being to handle this process. When you no longer put up a resistance, the knots will untie, and you will know triumph. Considering this, instead of merely identifying with the inner conflict, your being latches on to pure self-observation, making the most of this fitting occasion for transformation and healing.

What is the essential principle of healing? When we apply reason and observe fully and deeply, we see its effectiveness in every possible situation we can imagine. The healer, who joins in gratitude and is connected to health and Life, does not place his focus on the disease because he knows that this vibration would raise a barrier to the cure he proposes. The mere memory of a need connects us instantly with its vibration. This is one reason the Masters of this world chose to practice detachment, renunciation, as examples of their fruitful legacies. It is worth remembering the reasons that led them to choose lives without material goods; nevertheless, they walked as providers of all things, valuing Life at all levels. Again, the slightest reminder of need generates a change of mood that alters the state of consciousness, reducing the higher frequencies that sustain the being. The moment you choose to serve Life, your intent creates a situation of comfort, well-being, and enthusiasm enough for this blessed mission to triumph. If Jesus, Buddha, or any of the many masters had stopped to think where they would get shelter, food, and perhaps a little bit of understanding, they would not have been able to fulfill their magnanimous mission of delivering to the world the cherished truth of Love.

The relationship between the essence of your being and the *context* existing in each moment is one of the main reasons humans forget their primordial quality. The soul's essence is always present in the background of reality, a web of absolute and energetic information, although the human condition perceives this in a limited way. Yet, it traverses humans' existential processes through their consciousness.

As a social custom, humans have become used to a certain conditioning, acting in accordance with the active context in which they are inserted. Before long, patterns and tendencies emerge. Identification with the context is common practice, conditioning perception and mind to act on the level established by the conditions of such circumstances within the established boundaries. For this reason, in a family context, people fight with each other for their own reasons according to the set of beliefs permeating that environment. However, when one party relativizes their experience upon coming face-to-face with another vision of reality in a different environment, depending on their nature, they may open their field of awareness to broader information about life than what they had cultivated in their own home. At times, their foundational arguments no longer make any sense, while in others, they are simply expanded. However, this effect can occur at the same or greater intensity in those who delve deeply within themselves, changing their perspective.

Human beings have a natural impulse to connect. What do you connect with? Genuine confluence with the essence makes it possible to relate to human contexts without the need to self-exclude; instead of going within and seeing them as walls, embracing them through this essential awareness becomes the more beloved choice. Spirituality considers and respects the manifestations of all human contexts, considering free will toward current circumstances and the long history of everyone involved, so that all constructive spiritual interactions may bear fruit according to each person's current conditions.

The inner state of love and presence comes closest to the universal essence within our experience. Through wisdom, the nature of a context is recognized by immersing oneself in it, and at the same time by not limiting oneself to it. Therefore, one can move through everyday contexts without identifying with them. Connected instead to the flow of life, encompasses those daily concepts through a broader perception that makes it possible to receive information and energy in the consciousness, capable of transmuting and clarifying those environments, whether through words, new actions, or only with a peaceful presence.

People take the customs of the contexts they live in so seriously that children are handed *primers* at birth, containing the information they theoretically must know to participate in society. Delivered by parents, family members, teachers and other acquaintances, the primers teach all the standards that they think must be learned. Many doctors, teachers and professionals still hold on to them even in adulthood. At times, seventy or eighty years later, they will continue repeating the content of those models, checking to see whether they are acting accordingly. We would probably find it funny to see people hauling those primers around with them, folders and documents containing strict paradigms to be followed. We might laugh our hearts out.

This would help us see just to what extent many people live by the primers. What would happen if they noticed the standards they repeated from their parents, doctors, and teachers, in ardent confusion, all printed on sheets of paper that they carried along with them, consulting them constantly to copy them? It might be comical. Imagine them holding their folders close, so they could consult them every second, "what should I do now?" However, this is what happens, in people's minds and emotions. In this state, the ego ends up developing mental primers that are constantly consulted. Can you see how it is the same thing? People carry primers that most of the time are not on paper, repeating them incessantly, in some cases like machines and instruction manuals.

What is freedom like for you? You see, children do not like primers at all. They like freshness and flexibility, since everything is new to them.

From the nature of the child emerges a healthy openness to the joy of each moment's newness. Children are marvelously egocentric, true to themselves, at least until taught otherwise. At that stage, individuals inherently do not deny themselves, what they feel or choose. What is called egocentricity can be broadly reconsidered. The root of the word means being centered in one's own self. Where else should it be? Children are egocentric because they actually live in the world around them with open eyes, not the world imposed on them up to that moment. It was the primers that restrained our unimaginable and possible freedom.

Egocentricity is inherent to human nature. Nevertheless, children are yet unaware of the celebrated truth, that they are not the only ones with egocentric characteristics, that everyone has them. It is a profound task of the consciousness first to identify and get to know the existence of your own "I." Then, with effectiveness and respect, understand the existence of egocentricity in each individual besides yourself, before finally including all people, beings and forms of life as being present in the participation and constitution of your "I," in an act of connection.

Confusedly, people tend to say that an egocentric person is someone who only worries about themselves and harms others in the process. Then, when they want to follow their own feelings, they feel guilty. They ask, "How can I follow what I feel, my intuition, if others are pointing me in a different direction?" Many of us have been taught not to trust ourselves. However, every human being is essentially egocentric in the *good* sense of the word, since every individual is a potential being, in other words, they are egocentric, starting with themselves. We have made this into something terrible, as if being egocentric was against nature and even harmful to others. It is actually due to the imbalance in an *immature egoism*, in which one is not self-aware and does not respect others' egocentricity. This is a mission for a being's evolution, the possibility of maturing the ego's scope, from a state of apparent separation to a unified state.

Being egocentric and self-interested are not the same thing. On the contrary, they are completely different, near opposites. Egocentricity exists in those who follow their own self. Someone who is self-interested is always interested in getting something from others to fulfill their own self, someone who sources their own resolutions from others, just taking advantage of them. This kind of exclusionist interest only exists in immature egocentricity. Clearly, all people are endowed with interests, however, we tend to cultivate them healthfully when both involved parties agree, in full consent.

Being egocentric in the best sense of the word does not mean taking advantage of others or denying them; it translates to respect for your own self and others. What sounds more beneficial to you and everyone else? A world full of people who respect all forms of individuality? Or a world full of creatures that condemn the existence of an "I," that center their needs on others? A world of people who are whole or a world of people who are needy? Neediness is a demand to fill an inner void with something external. It is no surprise that there is so much lack in a world where we repeatedly deny inner experience. Authenticity becomes relevant. How could someone help their neighbors, lend a hand, if they had not done the same for themselves? Genuine generosity comes from someone who is consciously egocentric, because someone who helps out of obligation, just because they were led there against their will, or with the sole intention of garnering attention, is only pretending. How much energy would they channel into assisting others? A mature egocentric is someone who, when they do something, they do it wholeheartedly because it is a choice that comes from within.

There is a popular saying for those who lose part of this autonomy, "Someone who follows the crowd." This saying refers to an easily influenced person who goes along with other people's opinions instead of following their own heart. What is truly relevant here is not that you are following the crowd, but that you are following the crowd and leaving yourself behind, ceasing to be who you naturally are and becoming only what the world tells you to be.

Siddhartha Gautama, the Buddha, though promised a kingdom and positioned as a prince, chose to abandon this commitment, all of his people, including his family (father, stepmother, siblings, wife, and son), to follow the path that called deeply. If he had chosen to stay, swayed by all the regalia and material wealth of a prince and future king — where he remained until the age of twenty-nine, we would not be here now, over 2500 years later, speaking of his existence. His grand contribution of wisdom to the entire world would not have been passed down to us. If he had stayed, he would have cultivated interests that did not satisfy his spirit. However, because of his *mature egoism* he chose his own path over the highest influences and the attempts of others to prevent him from moving towards self-realization, touching countless souls for centuries thereafter.

It may seem paradoxical, but it is precisely respect and admirable egocentric maturity that allows for healthy cohabitation between humans and other species. A widespread lack of self-respect creates many problems in our shared world. Every individual, upon knowing themselves, changes that, maturing the use of their own mind. Many authors, scholars and observers of the human mind have cleverly dealt with forms of ego immaturity, making it possible for everyone to increase their awareness. Therefore, it is worthwhile to not make the ego into a villain or enemy to be condemned. But instead, let us, at the individual and collective level, open the field so the ego can mature as an instrument, so that it can become a space enlightened by the Being.

Someone who frees the ego from illusory barriers, allowing the whole of Life to embrace them, is like a bubble on the surface of the water that is entirely taken by oceanic fluids when its contour dissolves. When we are free, observing our neighbors as ourselves, our choices are mutually beneficial. When egocentricity is brought to maturity, we comprehend that doing good to our neighbor is also good for us, and vice-versa. When you follow the bliss of your being you are automatically saying to others that they also can. Both the greatest and smallest of human accomplishments are constructed through interdependence, the natural link of Life. Suddenly, it becomes possible to understand that the primers hindering our freedom were precisely what brought fear and violence upon us. Before that, you were free. We are free.

When children no longer want something, they do not think, "I don't want that anymore," or stare at it in dislike, pondering over the fact that they no longer appreciate it. They will even turn their head away, not wanting to strengthen what is now irrelevant to them. When children are closer to their innocence and away from primers, they simply cast aside what does not serve them and look at the new, opening themselves up to the now. They do not pay attention to what they no longer want, but lend their attention to the new that awaits them. Look at the world with the wide eyes of a child and you will find that wisdom.

Children see thousands of vehicles passing by, or even more — millions, billions, infinite vehicles crossing. Each serves as transportation to a new destination, just like cars, buses and planes, but these can go much further, since they are vehicles of possibilities. It is the same with the Universe, infinite in its multiple forms of transportation to new possibilities. Every one of us chose the primers to which we delegated the power that limits the probability of recognizing a new destination, here and now. It is worth pointing out that changing choices is present in the now, eternally.

Children enter a room and do not see it. They enter the forest and do not understand it. Whatever the environment, they do not see it. That is because, before they see the description given to things, before they enter the realm of words, they experience an atmosphere of creativity and ecstasy, of infinite perspectives. In that state, they are resplendent and jubilant about what is new in front of them, recognizing an indefinite universe. Fortunate are those whose eyes sparkle like those of children and who know a transparent mind like that of the little ones. Those who awaken in the light have the purity of children, the wisdom of an elder and the balance of a mature adult. There is no spiritual path without childlike purity, since this is the sustenance of the wisdom that is to come.

Children are completely attentive to whatever arises, open to the natural flow of change and newness. Their state is one of beautiful enthusiasm for whatever the moment brings. It is comparable to opening a present. You receive it and festively unwrap it. A child receives it and opens it joyfully. After all, is not this moment our present?

# CHAPTER 14

F amily is one aspect of human relationships that has a strong influence and guiding quality in the course of one's passage through existence. Recently, like never before in humanity, changes to general family structures have been taking place on a large, unprecedented scale.

Historically, families were rigidly structured, as if they were closed systems. A few families connected to financial power defined a great many societal policies. In many cases, they chose to use this power over other members of the populace, creating inequality. The only purpose of these few and "powerful" bloodlines was to protect their own families and structures seeking to increase their power. Unconcerned about other congregations of humans in their diverse world, they only looked out for their own. This was a common occurrence in practically every country around the world. Families expanded by force through war and conquest, even into territories considered to belong to other countries or distant civilizations. Those were times of great wars and conflicts.

Such families led empires, kingdoms, colonies, presidencies, and religious structures. In those times, family systems were very closed off. Sons were supposed to follow their fathers and let them guide their choices. The same was true for mothers and daughters, though, at times, the roles were reversed. Successors had to fight to uphold family traditions and, depending on the system to which they were introduced, it often meant deliberately harming people of other bloodlines, manipulating them to their own advantage.

Fear reigned in those days. Few sons or daughters dared to seek their freedom in the midst of such oppression. Children were raised with the expectation that they would become whatever their parents and predecessors chose for them. Most of the time, parents never learned how to choose for themselves, let alone for their children or an entire nation.

In the matter of relationships, countless marriages were arranged against the wills of those taking the vows; they were merely agreements between families equally powerful and influential, or at least socially compatible. How many had to endure a lifetime married to someone chosen for them, based on social obligation alone? How many must have tried fleeing with someone they truly loved in search of a peaceful life? Divorce was not even remotely possible; it was almost considered a crime. Once you married, you were tied to that person until death do you part, like it or not. Otherwise, you would be subjected to harsh prejudice, and nobody else would ever marry you again.

Relationships based on blood ties were considered a priority, and this kept family structures very closed. Throughout history, countless atrocities have been carried out in the name of blood relatives. Parents were endowed with great power. Someone in the role of father or mother had unrestricted authority over their children. Those who were raised by parents were merely pawns, pieces of property. The hidden wheel that used to rotate around this axle persisted because the parents continued the treatment they had received as children, perpetuating a cycle of deeply rooted consequences.

Today's society still feels the extreme consequences of these actions. However, even after so much conflict, these marks have left society with a significant legacy. By looking at these historical events from a reform perspective, we can truly appreciate freedom without needing to experience them again. Those were times that helped humanity gain experience and mature. Currently, amid globalization, deep changes are underway regarding the choices families make when organizing their structures. In the same way, it is worth mentioning the greatness of the choices for an individual who questions their experience regarding their relationships. Will they follow in their family's footsteps or will they, by renewing their dreams, choose to make changes to the direction that leads them where they mean to be in the world and family, opening new paths for those to come?

In some ancestral, integrated societies, upon birth, children were entrusted to the care of everyone in the group, especially the ones who had wisdom to share. Sometimes one or two years would pass before they received a name. It gave everyone a chance to witness the child's behavior and events involving them. Based on observations of the young one's personality, they would receive a name, often related to nature analogies. As they grew up, they would spontaneously choose their own parents based on degrees of affinity. Other times, as grownups, they had the choice to change their name. The view regarding families among different peoples appeared to be quite different from the one we have inherited to this day. It is all the more evident that this is not inherently a rigid system, but one that was designed.

Although changes have taken place many distortions in parent-child bonds still exist. We might add that exaggerated pressure is placed on the social roles that define what it means to be mother, father, son or daughter, not to mention grandparents and other levels of family relations. The models that shape these roles are in crisis, in a process of transformation. Children frequently grow up to repeat their parents' characteristics, oftentimes contradicting themselves in confused dissatisfaction. Then there are those who, instead of repeating them, do the exact opposite. Additionally, many parents do not manifest who they really are, they are content with living their children's lives, as if they could choose for them. In fact, some spend their whole lives trying. Instead, they can facilitate their path through a more beneficial connection, and even be friends. However, many parents still project their wants onto their children. This is a recurring theme in regard to their professional lives. Nevertheless, interference in one's choices commonly occurs among people who live together, changing destinies and their whereabouts. There is even a popular saying that goes: "Do as I say, not as I do." An obvious, but rarely admitted to, contradiction.

Long before children listen to what their parents say, they notice what they do, though they might not fully comprehend their behavior.

Living by example is the best influence in relationships. Moreover, it is futile for parents to try to prevent their children from seeing the world. When the parents continually try to inhibit their children's behavior, the children stop telling them what they really want because they know they will only be belittled. The children then will look for alternate ways to express their desires. Better for parents to consciously, joyfully and fully live their lives and share with their children those challenges and mysteries of existence they have learned about.

As parents raise their own consciousness, they will seek to interact with their children during the child-rearing years, passing on the most genuine values they have learned in life. It can happen through conversation or by listening attentively and respectfully observing where their children are in their development. Perhaps the main values are taught when parents encourage their children's freedom, to seek out their own values through experience as they find their own way, instead of becoming emotionally and psychologically dependent. A conscious parent's energy surrounds their child's experiential atmosphere.

With the intention of fully being a father or mother, coupled with a sincere desire for our children's well-being, come responsibilities that can contribute to their development, such as providing safety, nourishment, meeting their basic health and hygiene needs, caring for and protecting them from the elements, among other experiences belonging to the beautiful adventure that is this relationship, until the children can provide for themselves. All children require attention from different individuals, either from their parents, their guardians or anyone else who helps out, until a given moment. Love, applied affectionately, respectfully and joyfully, brings parents closer to the young ones. It is through this energy that parents clearly demonstrate the essential foundations the children will continue to learn through experience. When we say "close," we do not necessarily mean a physical closeness, but the true, inner and most subtle form of relationship between spirits. Over time, love will allow parents to discuss the circumstances that arise from experience, providing the strength that embraces the many particularities each situation contains. Happy are the parents who continue learning about themselves since they can provide their children with something even time cannot rust.

Children are living beings and have minds of their own. More than just a son or daughter, they come into the world as sisters or brothers on this life's journey. Instead of treating them as someone who does not know, treat them as someone who is in the process of remembering. Conscientious parents facilitate the development of those who are just starting over. Parents like these can perceive the beauty of supporting their children and showing them freedom, since love is free. The children will not feel pressured, as human beings have historically been, but will have consistent support as they take their own steps, possibly being grateful to their parents, seeing them as respectful, friendly figures. Genuine gratitude on both sides of a lived experience is one of the most sublime records established between beings and their relationships.

In addition, parental responsibility for children – regarding their dedication and care, by virtue of development of awareness and physical conditions – extends until roughly 16 years of age. Nonetheless, we know about numerous particular cultures and specific cases in which this is not always possible, and we are aware that so many little children around the world lack this type of care. All the same, on a deeper level, human beings will see that no one is responsible for any other spirit. At most, they are responsible for the choices that affect them. The best parent and child experience is one of following a path towards transformation, transcending those social roles as they become brothers and sisters on the journey.

Jesus, around two thousand years ago, left home at a young age as soon as he felt impelled to start his own spiritual journey. In those ancient times of inflexible customs, a widow like his mother should have been cared for by her eldest son, who in this case was him. Still, Jesus left home to accomplish the work that would have the greatest impact on humanity. Although societal conventions dictated the opposite, Jesus traveled, going to the desert and continuing on to other lands, only returning much later, prepared to carry out his divine purpose.

Jesus' relationship with Mary had already taken on another nature. He demonstrated this when they came to tell him, "Your mother and your brothers are standing outside, and they want to speak to you." Jesus asked, "Who is my mother? Who are my brothers?" Then he pointed to his disciples and said, "Look, these are my mother and brothers. Anyone who does the will of my Father in heaven is my brother and sister and mother!" – New Living Translation – Matthew 12:47-50. In this situation, Jesus took the opportunity to show that true family ties are not consanguineous, but spiritual, expressing the importance of unity between all beings.

Despite this, and even today, if someone close is facing difficulty, the vast majority of people will ignore them, pretending not to see or hear, just because they do not consider them family. However, when roles are reversed this same idea tends to be seen differently. Blessed are those who help anyone they can, regardless of any existing ties. So, here is a proposal that might encourage comprehension and education for the mind – to bring us closer to unconditional love. We can see all our neighbors, friend or stranger alike, as if they were our own child. If this is too difficult, as if they were our own brothers or sisters. This behavior of the thought systems provides, instantaneously, countless transformations. As a practice, it can modify any mental behavior, since people tend to think the best thoughts for their children, desiring all the best they can imagine for their experience, helping that being's choices to be welcome in the world. That is the tendency. It is no accident that from one incarnation to the next spirits shift between these roles, letting them create new spiritual ties, in some cases to ones they used to consider enemies. Living under the same roof and cultivating the same blood line does provide an opportunity for self-renewal, even while it may still be based on the widespread belief that they are now family.

Our society is undergoing a process that provides for new family configurations no longer restricted to consanguinity as more and more families are being fostered mainly by affinity and reciprocity. While blood ties will certainly continue to exist, the family structure will now be open and based not on traditional obligations, but on the naturalness of love. Families will no longer be formed by people bound by consanguinity, who only endeavor to protect their small group from others. They will be comprised of people united by bonds on many other levels of being. The day is coming when many will look at our history of separate and exclusive consanguineous families as a distant past, a time when love connections will not recognize boundaries.

Nowadays, many transitions are underway. The freedom to get

married or not, to live together or apart has broken historical patterns, which are now more open than ever. Many feel frustrated about having several relationships: they get married and then divorced. They still view these relationships as failures. That is a consequence of the earlier periods we have been discussing.

All relationships have had the proper time since there is no set time for them. They can last a day, a few months or years, or nearly an entire life together, but they are all long enough to serve as an experience. Time is not what defines them. The essential point lies in each moment lived, in what we make of it. On other levels we never stop relating to one another. You are not forced to find someone who will spend the rest of their life with you, no matter how likely this is to happen. There is no rule about this. If it were a natural law, it would always come to pass. Each relationship is an abundant field of possibilities for your development, especially those that go deeper. However, difficulties arise from expectations about relationships, which have been a source of frustration for many that later became a disappointment. Those needs are a still a consequence of what is in most people's subconscious.

We may or may not live with someone for a long time, side by side in a deep lifelong union. There is no right or wrong recipe for this. Nevertheless, it would be better for us to live each moment as if it were singular – as they all are. Instead, some people try to "hold onto" the other just to keep them perpetually in the future, while they stop living the here and now, making the most of those singular and fleeting moments. It does not only occur in marriages; fathers, mothers and children repeatedly do the same, having relationships of ownership, friction and attachment. By freeing oneself from those illusory beliefs and basing oneself on love, limits disappear, and genuine relationships arise. Changing the meaning of these and other unconscious historical memories, will allow human beings to overcome the need to attach themselves to old family and relationship standards and structures. Knowing themselves more effectively will make more harmonious and crystalline relationships possible and open the doors to new visions about family.

The fact that each person is currently inserted into a family context happens for specific reasons. We are born and grow up among people we have chosen for our development, however little we may know this consciously. This choice occurs at the spirit level. Still, being born among certain individuals does not mean there is a deep affinity. In practice, there are many cases where this is not true. This is a natural result of human diversity and people's different moments. However, the choice is generally made because of the experiences that nucleus can provide. They can sometimes be considered (relatively) difficult, but they generate a field of experience for the required evolution. Occasionally, internal resistance carried over for long periods asks for those difficult contexts, so they may be dissolved. A dissonant environment might be purposefully requested and foreseen by everyone involved in the spiritual sphere, so the experience can lead them to discover the apex of harmony. Being born to a certain family does not mean we are inescapably tied to them, only that the stage of experience will provide the blessing of opportunities for spiritual evolution, as much for us as for the others involved.

We do not have to change anyone in the family where we find ourselves. We can only transform ourselves. Our choices are our responsibility, just as they are responsible for their own. Nevertheless, when fulfilled, all those who have some connection and proximity to our energy are intimately affected in a field of new possibilities.

In this framework, there are three levels of families. Our current generation and those to come are lifting humanity from the first to the following levels. The first is the earthly family, the blood relatives. Those who honor it while simultaneously freeing themselves from its limits will open the door to know the next level. The second is that of the spiritual family of mutually supportive beings who frequently collaborate on the same constructive evolutionary proposal, and who occasionally cross paths over the course of many lives. Many spiritual family members have been called angels, guides, or mentors, when not incarnate. Happy are those who connect to their spiritual family, as it provides unseen and unequaled support, along with all those who fill themselves with light. Those who know their spiritual family, understand their work extends to all creatures, since their service, although vibrating close to the conscious travelers, is meant to involve all beings, achieving the third familial level. We are all a single universal family.

# CHAPTER 15

Among life's transient events, relationships are the ones that affect us the most, because not only do we have a relationship with other beings but also with our own inner selves. It is interesting how we, as individuals, have two basic conditions regarding relationships. The first being a steadfast connection to other human beings throughout our lives. The second condition, no more or less important, is that we appear to be alone so that we may live; after all, we are individuals. That statement might sound contradictory, but upon a closer look, we see that it is complementary. You are the All, what comes from you is another self, while I am another you.

Most individuals believe that they should stay close to others, invariably needing someone nearby, while others prefer to exclude themselves completely from the surrounding world, living solitary and isolated lives. Somehow, the other side always ends up attracted once again, reemerging. It is meaningful for us to understand that both conditions can coexist. Instead of denying our inner experience or setting ourselves up in opposition to our outer experience of coexistence, we embrace both in a healthy way, while they become one. We may be part of a crowd, but we are still individuals. Even if we seem isolated, nothing is separate. We all sprung from the same source of oneness.

It is common for beings to feel incomplete in the course of life. Perhaps you have been through this before. Have you ever felt incomplete? Have you, perhaps, felt as if something was missing inside?

When we deny our intrinsic movement, we lack something that is innate to us, therefore we project that need onto others so that they become the source of what we deny in ourselves. It could be your mother or father, principal or teacher, a friend or anyone else. You then project your need onto your neighbor, hoping they will provide what you need; it happens most often in romantic relationships, between couples. People look for someone, a companion with the qualities that will supposedly meet those needs. That is how we created the myth of the soul mate—that each person has a "better half" that completes them.

In this way, we create structures that demand that our needs be met from the outside. Many relationships are filled with expectations and demands that result in frustration time and time again. More than a few people become addicted to these imperceptive patterns. These individuals are quick to think, "That just wasn't the right person for me, I'll have to keep looking." We go from relationship to relationship, exhaustively searching for someone to complete us. That is, of course, when we do not wall ourselves off after suffering disappointment in our intimate relationships. The question is, is it better for two half individuals to be together or for two whole individuals to be united?

Soulmates do exist, but differently from what the cliché states; soulmates are numberless since all beings are soul mates and complementary in the only Soul there is. Nevertheless, over the course of many incarnations, some become closer to our experiences. There are those we meet over and over again. However, this does not mean we are bound to anyone, or that we are incomplete halves. There are countless cases where two or more spirits decide beforehand to find each other, so they can accompany each other on determined journeys, although, it is not always in the same way.

When needy states, tending towards impulsiveness, in which feelings of insufficiency and necessity are combined, are allowed to take over the mind, they can quickly alter our life's path, distancing us from our being's original objectives. Although this neediness may be far from the fullness of your being, spirit uses everything. Neediness is a feeling of incompleteness, together with a need to fill the void with something external.

When we cultivate relationships based on neediness, we are like a man or woman who believes they have lost the key to their own home. They stay locked out of their home, forgetting the fact they have the key somewhere on their person, in their pocket. They become temporarily homeless or they start looking to other people's homes for shelter, a place to live. Simultaneously searching, somewhat madly, for their own key in the places they visit, even though they had not been there before. Not unlike the individual who deems it necessary to take from someone else what they already have within, right under their own nose. If you open yourself sincerely, you will see it.

Relationships are natural to our experience, giving us an opportunity to express ourselves. There is no need to feel any kind of lack. What feed these emotional voids are precisely the scars and marks left by relationships, enduring over time. But even before that, what generates them is a lack of love for our own inner environment. The wisdom to clearly observe your own emotional states, as well as the details of your mind's illusions, is a valuable attribute in dealing skillfully with the emergence of such voids, which are still so common. The capacity to discern and clear up internal spaces emerges through self-observation and the sincere witnessing of oneself.

The spirit has no need for specific people, just naturally occurring relationships. No human being or anything else belongs exclusively to anyone since we are all free. Ownership is not ordained. If we do not even own our own bodies, which we know are impermanent, how could we own anyone else? In fact, nobody owns anything, we are merely in transit, changing, just as everything changes. No one truly rules over anyone else. If someone does not want to be in your company, do you want them to be with you, solely out of obligation and ill will? That is obsession, not love.

Happy are those who are fulfilled just because they live since they have no need for specific relationships and only relate to others through love. Fortunate are those who are together spiritually after having chosen to join paths; do not allow ownership to distort the emergence of such a gratifying bond.

Let us allude to the same idea by using a simple math analogy that will help us understand that everything that strives towards unification multiplies in the Universe. When you multiply two half people, you get one result: ½ x ½ equals only ¼. But multiply two whole people, and you get a different result: 1 x 1 equals 1. When two are whole, everything becomes one.

Considering the multiplicity of choices and human experiences, we are discussing not only the basic principles of marriage, gender irrespective, but also the pursuit of a path without romantic commitments, for those who choose to follow that path. Both are recurring choices in everyday existence, among the many who, deep down, only search for love.

The moment we understand the Love of the Universe, we stop begging for it, since it is a treasure always available. Observe how the All relates to you. Could there ever be a more beautiful relationship? Life gives you free will, respecting your choices; it grants opportunities, rejoicing in the diversity of experience. We say that God is Love, and to be one with the Universe means to be Love by nature. If the Universe acts this way with us, can we do the same? Since the universe has given us freedom, will we extend this to our neighbors? The universe has also imbued us with opportunities, will we share them? We are all crossing paths, expanding consciousness in formidable states of joyful relationships. See the Goddess or God in your companion. Treat each other as beings of divine substance—clearly and respectfully.

Every being is a vast and profound universe, *far beyond appearances*. When we free ourselves from social roles that prescribe stereotypical standards of coexistence, may we choose, together and on our own, to share such an enriching experience. Whenever two people come together with edifying purpose and true feelings, inexhaustible forces move together. When two become one, consciousness emerges to lend unconditional support.

Romantic connections can be harmonious when two people no longer desire to use each other. Many people enter into relationships with an agenda of their own, to gain something from the situation, with expectations, hoping for something. They might be material, financial, social, or sexual objectives, based on physical appearance, social status, general neediness, dissatisfaction, or a fear of being alone. While these reasons exist, they are ephemeral. We often see people who once professed to love each other, they now hate each other, engaging in mental, verbal or even physical battles. In fact, these individuals did not experience love in its entirety. Instead, they projected needs that were not met, causing them to rebel. When we say that we suffer for love, we are reversing causes. Love does not cause pain; it is the momentary lack of love in oneself that causes pain. Genuine love is not concerned about the way a relationship will turn out since it is only concerned with its own unconditional experience.

If we love out of admiration, our love ends when the other person changes. If we only love beauty, love ends as well when the other ages. If we love for security, when the other fails us, our feelings end. If we love for wealth, when that is gone, so is the love. Since our love is conditional, fear appears once again. Let us simply love the love within us, that we may come to love expressing our love. What would you do if you knew about the possible existence of a feeling that would never result in frustration, one that leads to communion with the source of Life?

When we choose to live our relationships with any conditions or demands, eventually, it leaves its marks on everyone involved, bringing suffering. No coexistence can remain healthy in the presence of demands. If pressure or any other type of control of the other person's choices exists, there is no peace.

Betrayal, much discussed and feared by so many relationships, is a personal matter. People do not truly betray their partners based on a personal attitude towards their partner; rather, it is often the result of confusion and the beliefs of supposed needs; betrayers mostly hurt themselves. Still, suffering spreads when everyone believes in the illusion that they can inflict the pain of disloyalty on others more than on themselves. The reality is that they are only inflicting more harm on themselves.

Do we need to search for reasons to forgive someone perchance? Must the other person prove something first? Do they have to be worthy of forgiveness? Observe yourself. Which beliefs lead someone to become so demanding? At times, there is no reason to forgive, while at others, it might be that we do not understand the other person's world entirely, or how they made their choices. First and foremost, just forgive them for yourself. While someone else may appear to have harmed you with their actions, you are the one who continues to relive it, by your own free will, living a story repeatedly inside yourself. Forgive yourself, and you will naturally be able to forgive the other. If you live in peace, you will truly desire peace for the other. This does not mean you have to try to forget, or pretend something did not happen. Instead, allow self-transformation by opening yourself to the state of forgiveness; it does not mean you allow someone to harm you, either; rather, it means no longer empowering the attitudes of others who would control your own inner state. Whether or not you continue to live with the people who may have hurt you in some way, inner forgiveness is alive inside you and is liberating.

The mind always needs a reason to love something or someone, making it a conditioned emotion. The soul is unconditional love. Essentially, there are no exclusive reasons for beings to love, since they *are* love and experience it naturally. However, the mind clamors for reasons to love, such as my child, my mother, my friend, my home, my pet, my girlfriend, my husband, or any other aspect with which the mind resonates. The greatest disturbances to coexistence arise when people identify with the idea that their partner belongs to them, a piece of property.

When the mind understands that love is independent of the other or any other sense of possession, that this sublime feeling does not rely on anything specific to awaken, but, rather, that it flows from the source within, then the mind will finally accept love as an inherent state. When the mind truly understands that we are one and that everything and everyone share the same nature, it brings love into every relationship.

Instead of going into relationships thinking about what we can get out of them, what we stand to gain from our commitment, let us think about what we can add to the relationship. All relationships, whether between spouses or casual encounters, are life opportunities for self-expression, an occasion for us to know ourselves and others, a fertile field waiting to be sown and a bountiful harvest in communion. May we make the most of relationships to manifest who we are, at the same time accepting the self-expression of our companion.

Healthy dialogue and respect for the other's choices are always welcome. The nature of love is not to wish for your partner what you think of or want for them, but, above all, to respect them, supporting their genuine will and the goals of their spirit before the existence.

Sex tends to be a somewhat misunderstood subject. For thousands of years we have transformed the experience into sin, vulgarity, violence and disdain, fear, and guilt, using it as a tool for manipulation and power. We have become used to feeling ashamed of our bodies, sacred instruments of Life. Nonetheless, the sexual act is the closest two individuals can become through the physical level. In renewed comprehension, clear communion is experienced by those who become one in the sexual act, not only in their bodies, but *especially* in their spirits, in simultaneous thought, feeling and action.

Sex, when imbued with love and respect, is the beauty of two people gently celebrating their bodies and the gift of union. Not as a means of satisfying an impulsive need—because it would never be enough, but by uniting in the simple expression of love, such a bond can reach a different sphere, as a moment of tenderness and sharing, allowing them to know more about each another. An act of surrender and appreciation, joy, and pleasure, contact and confidence, integration, and presence. Although the majority experience the sexual act solely as physical attraction, we have yet to know and live this experience deeply, stirring the energy of a relationship based on love, bringing joy to every level of the being.

If you choose to hold sexuality as sacred, when you are in a relationship, regardless of how long you have been together, observe whether you truly feel at ease on all levels, not just physically. When you feel attuned spiritually, mentally, and emotionally, in gentle, energetic synergy, your experience will likely be more complete. This feeling begins inside each one of us. When that is the case, you no longer worry about how often you experience sex, but only experience it when it comes from a spontaneous extension of love.

When we choose to be in a long-term relationship with the same person, and genuine inner feelings and spiritual lucidity are sustained, every moment is a new, different, and rich coexistence since each moment is unique. This experience can be one of the most gratifying ways to learn about ourselves. On the other hand, choosing a path of non-commitment between partners, as individuals, can also provide a valuable and unique opportunity to enter living consciousness. Throughout the different stages of our lives, occasionally, both possibilities may present themselves, if you accept them and make good use of them, each in its own time, they may prove to be very enriching experiences.

Those who find themselves spiritually do not reject or prohibit interaction with the opposite sex or gender they find attractive; they simply do not find themselves cultivating a sexual need any longer since they live immersed in the nature of love. Like a child who sets aside a certain toy as they grow up, not because they no longer like it but because they have played with it enough and now want to discover new aspects of their experience. It does not prevent their older selves from playing again if they feel like it, but, it is no longer a need.

We can liken it to the act of contemplating a hummingbird; we can look at the human beauty around us, merely rejoicing in it, without the desire to possess, just loving it. When we gaze at someone with the sole purpose of achieving an end like the sexual act or something similar, we are no longer present. And when another person around us serves as a motive to change our nature, for instance, through seduction, we waste substantial amounts of energy. Without opposing or resisting sexuality, one with self-mastery immerses himself in the Living Spirit, no longer feeling this or that need. In that state, such experiences are neither avoided nor needed, since they happen naturally in the confluence of love.

When you love someone, you are the one who feels that love; after all, the feeling takes place inside you. The person can be beside you or far away, on the other side of the world, but your feeling of love is there, coming to the surface since it is your own manifestation. You do not need that specific person to express your love, although this may naturally happen. The light of the other spirit can profoundly stimulate love and light in you. Many times, conditions along the paths of life can temporarily move us away from the people we love until we meet again. Allow yourself first to pour that love and respect on yourself and all things: from the smallest thought to a tiny flower to a child, to those with whom we share our daily lives, and even for someone who is far away.

In truth, for those in a state of unconditional love, meeting again becomes unnecessary, since there are no distances; unlike the conditional state, where beings in the illusion of attachment choose to share a home, even though both exist in opposite worlds, far from respect, truth, and love. In relationships of unconditional love, an unconditionally open mind has no reason to cry out to meet again since it is understood that the loved one is inside the one who loves, regardless of where they are physically, relating constantly to each other on other levels. When we love unconditionally, the mind no longer conceives the possibility of separation; if you live with someone in the same house, do you need to plan a meeting? The person is already with you, and so there is no such need. That is what happens when one achieves the nature of unconditionality. In other words, the loved one already lives with you constantly in your heart, and so there is no privation or the need to meet again since the possibility of need is no longer conceived.

One of the greatest interferences in relationships is the existence of assumptions. Assumptions are our tendency to believe we have to mentally suppose other people's thoughts, feelings, happenings, and choices, putting ourselves in their place as if we were the only ones there. Love, on the other hand, makes it possible to put ourselves in the other person's shoes as if they were them (which in fact they are), while still respecting the understandings and misunderstandings we can have about each other.

Many of us associate the idea of love with the experience of pain, accepting what we are taught, but is this association accurate? Some of us believe that for the other person to love us, they must suffer for us and that both sides should want to possess each other. If our partner does not seem attached and possessive, some begin to believe that person does not love us. The absence of jealousy, some would say, shows lack of care or concern. Are these nothing but beliefs held by the majority? When we choose these beliefs, we associate love with pain. Jealousy or possession has no place in love; when we taste complete love, we know those feelings are incompatible. Love is free.

Loving is a unique manifestation of each moment, across all space and time, allowing its energy to dance freely, vibrating throughout the Universe. When your truth spontaneously sprouts from your presence, and you feel free to be who you are and want to be, you respect the other's freedom to do the same. To love is to irradiate joy and peace in a way that words can no longer describe.

May we have faith, since, essentially, we all know love, our true nature. However, the present moment is the gift of knowing love in the opportunity of experience. May we allow Life to show us the Love that flows through us.

Let us love; not just as partners, parents, and children, but, rather, as brothers and sisters on the path of life. Love does not make demands; it is beyond the conditional, an unconditional state supported by absolute Love. There are no restrictions, and even though a relationship is a two-way street, love is found on all streets and begins with each of us. All the rest – restrictions, conditions and needs – is actually lack of love. We can say that love is the source that nourishes more than any food, makes more sense than any logic, and emanates more beauty than anything we have ever seen; love is in all these things— no more and no less. As we maintain ourselves in that state, we multiply it. When we love the All as we love ourselves, Life flows through us.

As Jesus put it long ago, *love your neighbor as you love yourself.* – New Living Translation – Mark 12:31. Perhaps, there is no phrase more complete than this one. Love your fellow creatures as if they were you, because they are. Nevertheless, even after two thousand years of difficulty in putting that maxim into practice, we may have something to contribute, approaching it from another angle. *Love yourself as you love your neighbor,* for many are those who, when they see someone in need, a beggar, an animal, a family member or even a stranger, suspend all judgment, expectations or projections and are moved to profound compassion and love, even for just a moment, facilitating resolution and healing. Still, there are moments when those same people do not display the same attitude toward themselves, falling back on the mind's illusions, demanding of themselves, as if they were the judges of their own consciousness. Consequently, let us use the same wisdom and suspension of judgment we oftentimes use with our neighbors and rest our own minds in the lap of healing by loving ourselves as we love our neighbors.

# CHAPTER 16

To this day, nearly every society is organized around a viewpoint of separation, which promotes fear of one another. The structures human civilization has developed itself upon, composed of a wide range of experiences, are under an intense process of transformation. Unmistakably, all of humanity has been changing from the very beginning, however, our current era carries the particular marks of its time. Many processes are happening at an accelerated rate so that the various changes in progress can be properly put into motion. No other period in known history has seen as many changes as the past few decades and centuries.

The world is changing profoundly. Even so, we know of the social difficulties that have existed and continue to exist in the world, such as inequality, hunger, thirst, violence, pollution, neglect, inadequate healthcare, obsolete education systems, among others. A range of experiences that might provide us the opportunity to know ourselves better. Still, we can see ourselves transforming such experiences as we change our deepest beliefs, thereby changing our reality.

While differences enrich humanity when they bring an abundant variety of positive experiences, inequality leads to self-destruction. Inequality frequently makes use of indifference, generating results like those observed around the world. Human equality generally makes use of diversity, such as the family that prepares different foods to fit everyone's appetites and tastes, and each member of the family is served accordingly. For instance, children do not necessarily eat the same food or the same amount as grownups. Similarly, equality does not mean everyone having or doing the same things; it means the opportunity to have or do what is deemed necessary. Whether people do things the same or differently, we understand that everyone has their own wills, and they vary widely. Free will is an excellent practical example since we are all free, but each person uses their freedom in different ways. Although people, communities, and countries believe they are unequal to one another, creating ideas of superiority and inferiority, and, even though we have classified ourselves as white, yellow, red, or black, the same human blood spills from the slightest cut to the physical body. Despite a great variety of classification schemes, all humans are *essentially* equal.

The entire planet is in a transition that has only intensified. And while so-called modern day humans are experiencing this unique moment, the generations to come will truly know how far we have gone. Initially, just like light defines a shadow, due to the information available and our search for consciousness, many circumstances considered negative will surface and become clearer, as has been happening. Hereafter, that distinction will allow new ideas to be embraced, and those spirits who choose to expand their consciousness will be able to make better use of their opportunities on Earth. The Universe has room for all choices, since we are all free, and this choice belongs to the innermost depths of each spirit.

The current systems of civilization known as socialism, communism, and capitalism, will not last forever. Instead, they are extremely limited because they carelessly use scarce resources in nearly all their relationships. And like previous civilizations, they will slowly unravel, making room for something unprecedented. These events originate from a separatist viewpoint, since, as a group, human beings still carry beliefs that create the experience of division, such as the existence of imaginary countries or conflicts with the natural environment where we coexist. These choices are creating an imbalance in the use of raw materials on this beautiful planet, home to countless beings. Climate change has been and will continue to be part of this framework of modifications yet to come, along with political, economic, technological, social, and systemic changes. What directions are these modifications taking? Spiritual changes are the foundation since they encompass all others. In times of need, some individuals will base their actions on the motto, "every man for himself," while others will lend a hand in solidarity with their neighbors until, eventually, most human beings will come to vibrate in a state of clarity. People will not enter identical states of consciousness, doing away with the wealth of diversity, rather, humanity is on its way to a never-before-seen general expansion of consciousness; each uplifting their own frequency.

Technology can be used more auspiciously, in ways we have yet to imagine, by balanced beings who are more self-aware and conscious of their surroundings. This is because technology is a projection of the human mind. Several means already in use can be refined into renewable and unified cycles that are more beneficial to humanity and the planet. Through inclusive choices made by human beings, unprecedented technologies and new sources of free energy will become tools for a brand-new configuration of the world.

New forms of education are progressively becoming established around the world, based on the knowledge of being, feeling, sharing, and integrating, completely reformulating educational systems. Gradually, instead of preparing children for future jobs that are constantly changing in the age of transformation, education can prepare them for life, knowing about the workings of the mind, body, and emotions. These academic proposals promote considerable changes—more motivating, clear and benevolent opportunities for the many spirits arriving to begin their journeys once again. Learning to look deeply at ourselves is a prerequisite to the development of a mature society. Regardless of the technique or ideology behind it, meditation is a common practice available to all for this purpose. Meditation encourages natural self-knowledge from an early age, connecting us with the wholeness of being.

As humanity chooses to learn about a world in harmony and peace, from the micro to the macro compositions, a revision by its citizens, from a new perspective, will shed light on its history. By observing and comprehending our history, we forgive ourselves and other human beings with the decision to learn from our experiences and not continue repeating what has become obsolete. The time has come for nations worldwide to ask for forgiveness for their past deeds, not just with words but with actions; religious institutions can ask for forgiveness for their past mistakes, and citizens from all cultures can share a global culture through new choices and new harmonious actions in a world that celebrates unity.

One of the main factors preventing societal structures from changing is internal— the individual's state of consciousness. We cannot effectively observe what is happening in society if we believe it is separate from the people who live in and construct it. States of consciousness have never been static; being constantly in flux and capable of expansion, though they may appear unchanging, if that is your belief. On a grand scale, each individual consciousness instigates the expansion of human consciousness, nudging it in the same direction.

Another factor holding the same structures in place is external, because many people in civilization feel basic resource insecurity. People in general are afraid of running out of food and water, or becoming ill without having anyone to turn to, or having to take a job they dislike to survive or receiving an education that does not prepare them for life. Some are afraid of fear itself, while others are afraid of losing their fear. When people are afraid of each other, they fear a lack of safety. And since we have chosen money to represent the value of our exchanges, many people fear not having money. On a certain level, the above insecurities originate from the internal factor.

Is there anything more symbolic than money? Those little pieces of paper can lead people to unexpected behavior—even kill for it! Tiny gold-colored pieces of metal? Our hunger for the color gold did not make sense to the indigenous peoples of the Americas, unless they considered the golden corn on the cob they fed to everyone present. Money, which has become almost entirely virtual, is an agreement between people.

Money is not good or bad since it is powerless on its own. Money is what you and I make of it. A large portion of humanity believes it is the solution to their problems, while another large portion believes it is the root of all problems. More likely, neither one is true. Money is simply a tool we use as we seek to reveal ourselves in our relationships (while we still use this system); it is an instrument of relationship, an object of exchange between people. It is a created opportunity, an occasion to relate to one other.

The issue is not how much money, whether a little or a lot, since we determine the relative value of an amount of money. Those perceived as poor tend to blame the rich and those perceived as rich tend to blame the poor. Who is to blame? Everyone? Clearly not, since in all matters *no one is to blame*; we are all individuals in a field of experimentation.

As you disincarnate, ending your experience as you now know it, nobody will ask about the number of material goods you owned or which social roles you played. You will only wonder who you really are, how much you loved, and how much good you did in your life. The best legacy you can leave in this existence is your own consciousness, having brought yourself closer to the excellence of love. Certainly, as a result, you will have left a natural contribution to the world. It can be splendid if we promptly move toward that level of loving consciousness within each of us, thus establishing a better experience for everyone.

As long as we live in a society ruled by finance, there will always be individuals who momentarily have more money, while others have less. It is up to human beings to choose to create other egalitarian systems. By intelligently creating balanced structures, where all people have access to quality healthcare, education, food, and sustainable energy—among other basic conditions, we not only eliminate current patterns but also build a bridge to the New World. The realization that we have the requirements—and always had—to proceed this way, bring a smile to our faces. In these improved conditions, millions of people awaken, one by one. Faced with a new awakening, you might ask yourself, "Where do we start bringing this new movement together?" In other words, "What will the road to this and other transformations be like?" If you are asking yourself where to start, begin by considering whether you are happy with the current standards or this new proposal is more attractive.

In many countries, citizens are waiting for their leaders to change the status quo, or to take stands that will transform society. However, every nation has the kind of government their collective consciousness embraces. Their representatives respond to the demands of the population's intentions. At the same time, others stopped waiting, having lost faith in politics, and spend their lives complaining about their leaders' failures. Still, others expect religious institutions or large corporations to transform society, while a final group waits and hopes for this to happen through military might.

How many have entrusted themselves with this change? We are in our comfort zone when we wait for others to change. At times, our psychological projection is so big that some of us come to the point of believing someone else's death might be the solution. Our minds tend to project onto external systems the attention and energy our own beings could use to create change. The transformation we have asked for in our civilization is for all beings to leave the comfort zone, and to enter a zone where we can freely express who we truly are and want to be.

Whatever situation you would like to change during your lifetime, always remember: *leaving what you want to leave MEANS entering what you want to enter.*

If you belong to an old personal system that no longer satisfies you, create a new one. Always start with yourself and your surroundings and expand from there. Be the better world you are longing to experience. If you have a business, transform it. If you work as a teacher, create, give your students space to create and think beyond repetition. If you work in groups, awaken their effective unity. If you are working "alone," awaken your whole being. Do not stop doing what you truly like to do, broadcast to the world what you feel, with dedication and attention, so that your achievements awaken individuals and stimulate the collective consciousness.

When you know within, and decide what inspires you to move in the world, the only thing left is to take the initiative, opening yourself to whatever comes up from time to time. Your personal mantra will be: What is the next step now that reflects my true nature? *One step at a time.*

We respect the doctors who need their patients' illness, the salespeople who need buyers, the judges who need injustice. We respect politicians' thirst for power, churches' need for congregations, and the competitors' need to defeat their competition. We respect a journalist's search for scandals, and a corporation's want for greater profits; in summary, human beings in all their correlations. In societal systems, structures are built on the foundations of what the inhabitants believe they need.

At times, a belief in the need for survival determines choices. Whatever the idea, it branches out inside the mind, until it is replaced by a better one, or it is given a new meaning from another angle. The idea of survival continues through fear, from the need to distance oneself from death. That fear allies itself with the belief of a finite existence. What is the good of living with others if life ends at death? What is the point of helping others if nothing remains? What is the difference between doing good and evil if both disappear? Many people have asked themselves these questions. As long as humanity does not remember the continuation of life and reincarnation by studying it and understanding it gradually, personally, and collectively, these beliefs will continue, driving some individuals to harm others in order to survive.

Human beings bear the need to be remembered by their loved ones and neighbors, even on the brink of death, since they feel, even unconsciously, the continuation of their presence and their feeling of connection. The idea of finitude contains the belief in separation, as if we were to become separated from the Universe upon death. However, in nature, nothing is lost. Continuation is a component of Unity, since we always have been and will be part of the cycle of the All.

Do you think people, like the previously mentioned professionals, would make the same choices again? Would they stop caring about humanity and the Earth if everyone knew they could return to it someday? Would they still have the need to see time passing, just to ascertain their survival? We reap what we have sown and renew ourselves by choosing new crops to grow over multiple existences. This opportunity is open to everyone, not some privileged. As the identity you know yourself to be today, you are unique to this existence, finite in this time and form. But for the finite to exist, something must be infinite, in this case, your consciousness, which is eternal.

This more holistic comprehension takes ideas in another direction, awakening the best in our being, replacing survival related fears with the emergence of love in every existence. When simply surviving is no longer the most meaningful part of existence (it has never been), new possibilities for deep meaning blossom, a better life for our being, through love. This choice carries your being's ecstasy to the entire Universe, through infinite forms. Belonging to eternity as we do, what could be more meaningful than making choices that fully reverberate with this immensity?

As a society, we are not usually clear about what love is, and we often are very far off the mark. Frequently, it is confused with expressions like sexuality, maternity, femininity, romanticism, and weakness, among others. But love encompasses strength and tenderness, masculine and feminine, friend and supposed enemy; it is in the expression of mother, father, children, and stranger. Love has no stereotype. There is no greater intelligence than love, reflected in unity, wisdom, truth, and joy. Love covers everything, including its own depth and breadth. Watch closely and deconstruct some of your preconceived ideas about this living manifestation.

We have created countless, never-before-conceived professions in recent centuries. How many more can we create under other prisms? More than the quantity, it is the quality that will make a difference. Let us create new, inspired trades, professions, and situations based on unity, veracity, and sustainability, illuminating each working environment.

Do this where you are, and others around you will follow suit. Conceive this new world. Doctors and other health professionals mainly using health as a tool for their promotion and work. Politicians no longer having power over others, but together with others. Churches no longer depending on their congregations or their congregations on them, nor do they follow competitive and divisive principles. Instead, they fraternize and share in unity and celebration. Competitors no longer fighting to defeat their supposed opponents, knowing that, essentially, they have always been playing with themselves. Games becoming an expression of being all one. Journalists no longer concentrating on scandals, but on solutions and creativity, through teaching and sharing. Internally committed to the truth, journalists' influence aid humanity in clarifying information. Each company being very clear about what their operations entail—expenses and profits—and everything being out in the open, with nothing to hide, electing transparency for the individual and common good.

Inevitably, the time will come when we will realize that perhaps one of the most illusory beliefs still held by human minds is that everything has a price. Interlaced with their daily ideas and attitudes, people carry around these financial concepts of charges, debits, payments, and gains or losses. Some say this is just how the world operates, but the world only operates this way because that is how we have set it up and promoted it. Life is not based on trivial consumption, as our systems have done with the world's resources. Left to itself, life works in unity with everything in the Universe, not through unconcerned and separatist depletion of its abundance. We were sold the idea that everything has a price, and we bought it. Nearly everyone bought into this belief since that is how we set up our society. Very often, these beliefs have even led us to sell people, using as a pretext the regrettable precedent of other cases of slavery. We have sold animals, water, and plants. Who determines the price of a life?

We respect humanity's different periods, even though we know that such collective systems and thoughts are impermanent. Nothing has an inherent price, not a single object. Not even silver or gold mines have their own prices. Prices are mental creations and illusions. Can we not sense the disparity of putting a price on everything? Can we sense the relativity? Has nature ever defined a set price for any realm? All the same, these concepts have spread to our daily attitudes as well. Many of us give, demanding something in return, while others give of themselves and demand to be rewarded. We soon get used to mechanically selling ourselves and buying something, or even someone. These fear-based structures have supported many pillars in our minds. Someone who senses that everything is based somewhere between love and fear, by choosing love, they will slowly become aware of what is simple and essential. Therefore, their journey among people will transcend conventions even further, becoming closer to truth and life.

The incongruent belief in prices is a human idea based on the illusion of ownership. Nothing belongs exclusively to anyone. Attempting to set a specific price for something is the same as expecting it to remain unchangeable. Nothing is truly "yours." Everything that has come to you will be taken away in time. Why? Because even your "temporary self" will be carried away by time. Nevertheless, the law of change is precisely why each thing or moment is unique to that moment in time; its worth is directly tied to its transitory nature, which denotes the singularity of everything that is, emanating the unique value of its presence. For this reason, in this complex array of so many inexpressible values, life is made sacred in the unity, where everything is interconnected. Resource depletion, buying, selling, and theft are separatist illusions. May we observe the magnitude of the law of the Universe that offers everything free of charge. Absolutely everything.

The first act that proves life operates in this way is free will, which was given to everyone. Nobody can put a price on our choices; they are literally *free* will. The power of freedom was given to us, free of charge; just like being born or the air we breathe, or the food provided for the birds and water for the fish. If human beings knew the value of life, they would see an astonishing difference between value and price. One of the reasons why humans have been experimenting with systems of prices and consumerism is precisely to perceive its contradiction. Through temporary coexistence with these deceitful and illusory "values," called prices, humans can come to understand life's inestimable value. Life's worth is inherent and immeasurable because it emanates meaning, energy, and existence.

Nobody pays a price for their choices unless they believe they must pay one. Nobody owes the Universe anything, nor is anyone the designated bill collector or self-appointed vigilante. We did not buy our existence. We are free to choose; we have been given that opportunity, now and always.

Very few truly understand that a single source lies behind all things. Some call it God, Universe, or other names, but everything comes from the All. You might not believe everything is free in the Universe because you do not believe in yourself and in Life. "Who am I to give and receive at will? Who am I to trust that much? Am I worthy enough to have full faith in Life?" It is what many people think out of fear since this has been the prevailing belief; realities have been built on that belief.

A lack of self-love is the reason you feel unable to surrender to the Universe. Fear makes us think that if we surrender to faith, something will go wrong, and we will once again have regrets, becoming embittered with Life. But faith has never meant closing oneself off through expectations that often turn out to be unfulfilled. It is not stubbornness or resistance. These reasons cause anxiety in so many hearts. On the one hand, when lacking full confidence in life, the mind constantly engages in games of expectations and attempts, fabricating risk and benefit agreements, similar to those learned in the execution of the widely disseminated business transactions. On the other hand, when there is full confidence in life, the individual comes to know what the expansion of consciousness is.

Every belief creates the experience of reality. However, at the level where beliefs abide we can find the existence of other multiple beliefs that intersect, sometimes in conflicting directions, interfering in each other as well as in their results. Faith, however, is an unrestricted belief, the highest level of wholeness of a single belief. Without any room for opposition, a belief that reaches the state of faith sees itself as unlimited in the sphere of the mind. In this state, it unites with the Universe, experiencing the power to create.

The Absolute grants you the ability to choose whatever you like. However, make sure your choices come from a sincere internal *decision*, together with your words, thoughts, emotions, and intentions. All our skills are brought to surface as far as we believe in them. There is no need to believe anyone who tells you that you cannot be in God's presence. You are right now! Look around you, sense life, feel it, she is in everything, in each and every single thing. You are a presence of God. Although there may be countless unseen and unheard events still shrouded in mystery. Still, only you can make that presence increasingly conscious, beginning with your own presence right now.

Believe, you are granted everything. Do you think if you ask for unity, it will not be given? If you ask for strength, it will not be provided? If you ask for prosperity, it will not be delivered? God can give you much more than that since everything is at your disposal, through you. Therefore, the best request is gratitude. What will God give you? In response to each request, you will be given an *opportunity*. If you ask for unity, Life will give you people and beings, so you might be an element of that unity. God will offer you the opportunity to exercise your strength, which will emerge from within, as water sprouts from a spring. According to the expansion of your consciousness, having the "eyes to see" yourself as an art in progress, you will come to see the magnificence permeating existence, interacting with everything and everyone. The time will come to experience opportunity of abundance with everything that is. At that stage, need fades away and only gratitude remains.

Attention is the greatest tool given to human beings. Focus your attention on something, and you will give it life. Whatever we focus on receives the energy we generate through our thoughts and emotions. We have paid great attention to fear in our lives, expressing it every day through concern for the problems we recreate every day. Most of us, habitually spend our days solving problems, meeting demands, managing gains or losses. At times, we lament the past and fear the future. At a certain point, usually as we climb into bed at night, we look back on a few moments of our lives, choices, and feelings through prayers, meditation or by reflecting about the reason and meaning behind the attitudes of that day. Frequently, by the end of the day, many are feeling confused and insecure. In an act of faith, we do the opposite, and we surrender ourselves to Life, carrying out actions in the sublimity of our being. We spend the entire day as in a *state* of prayer and meditation. In this case, full attention comes naturally, as if we levitated in our splendid feelings, stopping just occasionally to ponder what is going to occur, with commitment and faith in our actions. When we choose to live the best way we can, our daily result can only be one of excellence, even when facing adversity.

In that state, you do not count your coins or watch the numbers constantly as if something was missing, feeling insecure about your survival. You rely on God in yourself to achieve the goal and meaning you have chosen to express in this existence. Focus on the now, on the best expression of yourself at this moment, entrusting the rest to Life.

Prayer is not necessarily about repeating traditional religious phrases, mouthing the words mechanically. There will always be prayer in the simple act of bringing the deepest feelings of the spirit to the surface, using your thoughts, words, and actions as a genuine instrument. Meditation does not necessarily consist of assuming special positions, breathing techniques, or making certain sounds, rather, it is a meditative, contemplative state of spirit, connected to Life. Although both can be practiced in these ways, let us not confuse the method of transportation with the destination. Such states of surrender and connection can happen when sitting or walking, alone or in a group, aided with certain techniques or spontaneously. The vital point is the true intention and the actions that arise, according to the choices of the spirit, so that we might leave this life better than when we came into it.

# CHAPTER 17

Does life make a distinction between rare and common flowers? The human mind does. By only admiring the rare ones, as if they were more important, we neglect observing the more common plants around us such as grasses, and other herbs dubbed weeds and considered run-of-the-mill, though full of unknown, powerful properties and uses. Most of us do not pause to notice how a flower considered rare by one person can be commonplace to another, and vice versa.

By the same principle, many of us overvalue tasks considered uncommon or difficult. By creating realities around these circumstances, we neglect, once again, to observe everything life so readily gives us. The idea of the "hard-won" victory, so deeply ingrained in our culture, sustains suffering in our experiences. In consort with love, everything is unique and alive at every moment, making the human experience simple and gratifying. Abandoning beliefs that cultivate a need to make things difficult and create suffering means valuing and betting on what is most simple and abundant in ourselves. It is so simple it may seem unattainable, but is perfectly within our reach. This reformed attitude confronts suffering head on, bringing unfettered thoughts and feelings to the experience, shedding light on whatever makes us believe that difficulties are necessary. Life sees every flower as both extremely beautiful and common. How many of us, when seeing a plant sprouting from a crack in the concrete feel its vitality and resilience bursting forth, even in that inhospitable environment? When beauty arises from within, we see it in all things. Is your daily routine different, or is it just compassionately waiting for a new landscape to spring from within you, like a plant growing through concrete?

If a plant can sprout from the pavement, wouldn't your sublime actions also bear fruit as society charts a new course? To this end, we can modify another widely disseminated element—complaints. In some countries, one day a year, Thanksgiving is celebrated; it is a day dedicated to gratitude, which leaves the other 364 days for complaints. Just as we can walk without thinking, having made it an automatic action, we have done the same with the act of complaining. But unlike walking, which can be extremely useful, complaining is the act of creating and re-creating countless misfortunes, similar to a snowball effect. There is a common belief that lamentation is the inevitable result of unsatisfactory circumstances. On the contrary, it is what creates the energy to maintain them, making room for disagreements with life. Many of us are so *familiar* with complaining that we no longer notice we do it almost every time we open our mouths. What is more, when strangers are getting to know each other and conversation runs out, they are sure to find something in common to complain about. If we also take a look at the way our thoughts develop, constantly and silently, we can see that whining, about a wide variety of subjects, is part of the wonderings of the mind.

Many of us complain about the weather on hot and cold days, on rainy or sunny days. Some complain about the food we are about to eat and the clothes we are about to put on. There is grumbling as we wake up in the morning and sometimes when we go to sleep at night, even about the profession we have chosen. We complain about our family, teachers, or coworkers, and we have no fewer complaints about society, life, God, and ourselves. Have you ever thought what it would be like if we dedicated 364 days to gratitude, and just one to complaints? There would be nothing left to complain about, as great blessings arise from gratitude. Not a single minute of complaining is necessary for us to solve our so-called problems. Effective resolution is supported through awareness and clarity, by taking responsibility for our choices and connecting our state of consciousness to gratitude.

For most people, expressing gratitude has become an unexpected, out-of-the-ordinary event. This state of gratitude is so unusual as to become an event in itself when it happens. At isolated times of the day, something happens that gives rise to an infrequent, joyful exclamation: "Oh, I can even feel grateful for what happened today!" The marvelous act of thanking life can become a good daily habit: "Be grateful, just for the sake of being grateful." Even better than saying it is to feel it. Gratitude conveys no obligation or debt, only the clean, spontaneous, and unpretentious act of recognizing life. A way of requesting, creating, and manifesting, which is, in this state of grace, a constant, prosperous, and brilliant encouragement of all that is best in the life that surrounds us.

The state of gratitude is the mainstay of a harmonious consciousness and its peace and strength can naturally bring us closer to the *truth* by supporting it in our awareness. As we transform the basic beliefs that make up the human experience, we begin to deal with classifications, and the conceptions of right and wrong we have attached to the meaning of truth; these all become clearer when the spirit, instead of the mind, guides our consciousness. Absolute truth cannot be contained in models, concepts, images, or patterns. At most, when not illusions, they are only pale representations of life's truth. Absolute truth is, above all, beyond the mind and its flow cannot be contained. The mind only interprets it and channels it, after all, the mind lives in the world of relativity. Although we constantly swim in the waters of truth, we feel this majestic flow more intensely when our presence is whole and free of labels and established conventions.

You have always been and always will be free, like everyone else.

Freedom is not the same as being physically adrift in the world. It is not about being able to move around or the number of material things you own. Or receiving someone else's blessings for you to be free. Freedom means *being* free, from within. Being conscious of what you have always been. We hardly remember just how free we are, for all freedom comes with a "limitation" since we are not in absolute conditions. Nevertheless, we can either see the conditions we have chosen as limiting, such as our physical bodies, or as vehicles of opportunity. It is a matter of perspective. Essentially we are free, a state of being always available to the spirit.

Truth is the path towards freedom. In this case, speaking the truth does not necessarily mean saying everything that pops into your head all the time, but knowing the magnificence of being, first and foremost, absolutely true to yourself. The feeling of embracing this inner accomplishment is indescribable, and is everyone's right. Moreover, sooner or later, everything becomes clear. By not being true to yourself with your thoughts, words, and actions, by not listening to your deepest feelings, you shut yourself off, depriving yourself of the freedom and power of transformation. Human beings can always learn more about themselves than they ever thought possible, at any moment, in an unending process.

Truth is a designer of enigmas. As absolute, it has but one source, from which multiple variables happen. Originally, truth is what it was, is, and will be, forever. As has been said before, the truth will set you free. However, in human experience, truth appears as a transitory phenomenon of a temporary illusion since there is always another truth, broader than the one we have experienced. Such greatness only lives on an expansive scale. With eternity, there is always another infinity to embrace. The truth to which we aspire always comes with the unveiling of a temporary illusion. There is a bridge to consciousness every moment of Life. Truth and humility are our feet. To get us across the bridge, both of them say: "Walk with us, in yourself, and you will know who you are."

Therefore, *the most effective change, increasingly requested by human beings, rather than being political, economic, or social, is a change related to consciousness.* Naturally, our consciousness knows the paths of truth, expanding endlessly, freeing itself from limiting beliefs. Culturally, human beings have become used to feeling guilty, which only exists in their minds, for the time being. Guilt is not the fruit of something inherent. Historically, society's foundations have been based on beliefs that revolve around guilt. For millennia, we have repeated the idea that we are born into sin, embedding the idea of guilt into us. From guilt's perspective, there is no solution, as long as it remains attached to previous events, hurting us, always accompanied by self-judgment and punishment. To blame yourself is to punish yourself. Guilt is a dysfunctional form of regret. It is very common for individuals who feel victimized to also harbor feelings of guilt because they both use the same channel inside the mind. However, a new perspective makes the metamorphosis of these internal spaces possible. It is our responsibility to make the change.

The meaning of *responsibility*—in a lighter, more effective way— means making room for transformations, based on new actions which result in favorable solutions, bringing us to a renewed choice of the present moment. Certain dimensions of Spirituality no longer use the terms guilt and sin, replacing them with the word responsibility. To assume responsibility is to understand that we have the power to transform our reality through our beliefs and choices. Faced with a decision we would rather not make, *functional repentance* means taking responsibility for what we decide to change.

As long as we continue to think that we, as individuals, are not responsible for the events of the world, we uselessly continue to wait for things to change into what we would like them to be. Though we are not directly responsible for anyone else's choices, we are responsible for our reactions to them, every moment, and how we carry out our own. We are responsible for our state of consciousness and the creations we bring about. If we have made a choice that created unpleasant results for others, guilt is not a necessary component in making things better or transforming the experience. This would only complicate life's natural consequences for our choices. Effects will come about anyway, even when guilt persists, and are often intensified by the person's beliefs. If we decide to take responsibility, based on love, everything turns into bliss and healing. Effective change arises when people take responsibility for life as a whole, as a natural process, from within, and share it, not out of obligation or as punishment, but for the well-being of individual and the collective consciousness. There is no need for obligations and demands, since taking responsibility does not mean demanding reality from yourself at all; it is about entering a relationship with it, or even better, realizing that you are reality itself.

As an example, let us consider the fact that we still leave people we consider guilty in cells and prisons, or cases in which, as a society, we choose the death penalty to show others that killing is not accepted. What purpose does it serve, if there is life after death? If cycles repeat themselves? If the same energy remains and we do not make room for healing? While we continue to act this way, we should first notice the imbalance demonstrated in the number of people with reasons to be arrested (if the laws were strictly enforced, over half the world population would be imprisoned). Secondly, that we do not understand human beings enough to deal accurately with them and their current life histories, much less other existences. We would rather leave them in cells to forget or postpone the problems, while their numbers increase globally, since they are continually chosen, perpetuating the same cycles. Let us make new decisions and start anew, taking responsibility for a renewed world. We can form truly efficient systems with real opportunities for transformation, awareness raising and the extensive reintegration of beings, who are humans just like us. All we need to do is ask whether we would like to be treated the same way, neglected by all, or if we would love to face the possibility of healing and improvement since we are all one family.

Some indigenous and African tribes used to have efficient customs when dealing with members who had made mistakes that caused harm to others. The entire tribe got together and attentively, with great love, firmness, and awareness, surrounded the individual whose actions had created difficulties that were harmful to everyone, reminding them of who they really are. Instead of being engulfed in guilt, the person felt support and positively regretted their actions, feeling the desire to begin expanding their consciousness once again. Imagine if this custom were part of our current culture. The balance and fluency of energy moved by beings creates renewing instructions in those who are beginning their journeys once again. We are energy movers; let us not underestimate the power of our influence. If you have ever had a person that truly believed in you, you know what it is like. Be that person.

Believe, you can be an element of transformation, starting simply with your own life. Collective barriers are overcome by many people renewing their consciousness every day, inspiring people to take steps toward the New World. Under the intensive changes by every human being and their respective creations in society, such as relationships, professions, and basic living conditions, among other changes, new forms of living develop, yet unknown by the great majority of humanity. The doors have always been open for the creation of an effective world filled with wisdom and better opportunities; it is up to every human being to enter so that every system in effect can be modified. The moment humanity believes it can change and makes that choice, solutions immediately become clear.

The illumination of human beliefs is part of this process. From the moment we are born, we repeat what is shown to us as right and wrong. However, remember that the spirit consents to all these relationships, before and throughout your existence. In this case, from an early age, children are saturated with pre-established ideas, most of them originating from fear. When children naturally begin to manifest themselves, they find labels for what they are doing, indicating that for the most part, their choices are wrong. This leads to a fear of choosing, because so many of their actions have been labeled wrong from a young age, and so their being agrees to all those concepts, subtle or not, and stores them in hidden spaces of their minds. At this point, they still believe they can choose; after so much repression, some believe they no longer have the choice to take their lives in a different direction. Having believed that there are no choices, they experience that reality and end up granting the world permission to choose for them. After they tire of the recurring ideas, believing they made the wrong choices, their confidence and self-esteem are shaken up; this leads them to reflect on the possibility that something right exists, and they begin to look for it.

Who defines what is right? Parents? Schools? The government? Religions? The military? In the meantime, we discovered that what many considered be right is actually considered wrong by others, and vice versa. In a state of confusion, you asked yourself, after all, who is right? Either you continued feeling bad about yourself and believing you were wrong (about certain things, of course), or you decided that someone else's point of view is right for you. Everybody in society has gone through a similar process. The following will be music to many people's ears: there are no definitive prototypes for right or wrong regarding our choices. The Universe does not judge; it only creates with us. Perhaps we will continue to search for others who can tell us what is right until the truth that resides inside of us becomes enough.

By holding ourselves up to models of "certainty," many of us believe we will not feel bad about ourselves again, like we did at certain points in our childhood or other stages of life where we believed we were wrong. (Including unassimilated memories from prior existences, generally brought on by related feelings.) In order to continue upholding our own beliefs, many of us wish to suppress other people's certainties, which are so often contrary and incompatible with our own. We tend to group ourselves with like-minded individuals, to strengthen concepts that we believe are "correct;" at times, we try to portray other people's thoughts and words as wrong. Notice how most of us are not bothered by the fact that others believe they are wrong; however, many have felt bothered by their belief that they are right. If someone says, "I am wrong," many people identify with it subconsciously, at times, they are delighted with the situation since it can be a confirmation, in their minds, that now they are right. If someone else says, "I am right," or implies it in the tone of voice, many have a habit of feeling annoyed, irritated, angry, or mistrustful since this might imply that they are wrong—if there is disagreement in their points of view, bringing back unpleasant feelings. When we become aware of these mechanisms generated by the ego's unconsciousness, we no longer worry about the game of wanting to be right. There is no longer a reason to be part of this game.

Be aware that nothing has ever been right or wrong in your choices. Humanity was not handed out a manual of correct and incorrect behavior. There are only creations and expressions, choices that are conscious or not, each leading to their own results. That is all. Looking for certainty and mistakes means setting oneself up to follow models or recipes; to transcend such conventions is to become increasingly aware of your skills through creative responsibility. How will you feel when you no longer view everything from a perspective of "right versus wrong"? See for yourself. As individuals abandon the right/wrong conflict and the illusory need to be right, space opens up for choices with real certainty. Define your certainties to create your reality, because, at the end of the day, there is not an ounce of certainty in anything in the world. Instead, all the minds that believe to be certain about something create experiences accordingly. You will define your certainties by your choices. You can unconsciously accept other people's models of certainty, or use the strength Life has given all of us so that, through your certainties, you can create your experience of reality.

Beliefs and thoughts are the lenses through which we view the world. Respecting others' views allows you to express your own. Society makes room for different ideas; however, it is possible to respect these diversities, rather than try to prove that we can win and be right. Instead of trying to convince people that they are wrong and we are right, we can try to understand them, as part of our self-knowledge; understand that these concepts are only mental games and we do not need to play them anymore. We are all just beings experiencing cause and effect. Therefore, we do not say "the correct ideas for the world," far from it. What we are saying now is that *all* ideas create the experience of the world. Thought gives rise to *belief*, and a *chosen* belief becomes a reality. Then, what gives rise to thought? God, Life, Love, I/We, all the possibilities. What is a thought if not a possibility?

We often believe that the development of our beliefs happens in levels, that they follow a from-here-to-there scale, that they develop gradually and progressively. However, from the moment we believe in the gradual development of our beliefs as if they need more time, it becomes our experience. Our belief about the functioning of our beliefs shapes our reality, in this case, waiting, postponing. There is no set time for a change, other than the one you believe.

By observing a relentless, self-proclaimed atheist who does not care what other people think, we might see that, based on several aspects of their beliefs, they are in truth a person of faith. Because, even when people try to convince them of anything else, they remain strong in their convictions. They have no doubt the world is the way they think it is. Even though it may not be, that is how they experience it. Such is the power of faith; regardless of the form a belief takes, since there is no judgment coming from Life, it creates that being's experience of reality. Faith, of whatever nature, is the being's undoubting belief that transforms their reality.

The faith connection can develop gradually, if that is what the person chooses to believe in, just like they can believe that love is experienced, nourished, and known gradually in levels, from conditional (filled with attachment, passion, and worries) to unconditional love. There are no judgments, haste, or even preferences. The Universe accepts our choices since it has given us free will. However, if the same person believes in unconditional love and chooses it with the same conviction as they trust the act of breathing, they will immediately become immersed in it. Faith has this effect on anything people come to believe in fully, leading them to experience it instantly. When the person cultivates their energy and surrenders to faith, a deep connection with Spirituality develops, making it possible to act intensely at every opportunity.

Whatever we believe in with the same unshakeable belief placed in the act of breathing, in absolute faith that air is at our disposal, miracles occur, each according to the dynamics and nature of the belief. If we were to ask someone about to embark on a world tour if they had done research on the countries that have air to breathe, they would undoubtedly say, "no." Why? Because they are confident they will be able to breathe. There is not an ounce of doubt, only confidence.

Perhaps our greatest act of faith as human beings is the act of breathing, the certainty that we will always have air to inhale, without worry or hesitation. If we had the same faith about any of our other beliefs, miracles would occur. It is no coincidence that the lungs are a pair of the body's organs that mysteriously and most easily regenerates. In fact, there is no mystery, only the certainty that they will never lack air. It is no coincidence that many people feel a forgotten peacefulness in breathing, because they have never felt reservations or doubt about it, only the certainty that everything is perfect. Deep states of meditation are habitually achieved through breathing, not because it has that property on its own, but because it is in breathing that our being rests in the absence of doubts. Any other belief we fully trust is an act of faith that will lead our being to states just as intense as those experienced in the deepest meditation.

We can see how much our beliefs shape our reality by noticing that the heart is the organ with the strongest reaction to beliefs. You can find it in literature, poetry, and films, as well as in common knowledge— that the heart is the organ of most emotions, so that when people have strong emotional reactions, it deeply affects their hearts. Even during a sports match, a passionate fan can suffer a heart attack because of their intense emotions during the event. People place their hands on their hearts when they want to tell you their feelings. It is no coincidence that there are countless heart institutes and hospitals around the world that specialize in the heart. Medical science has done extensive research, so they might be able to recuperate, support and revive hearts. Because of the excessive emotional burden humans place on the heart, this organ has become susceptible to oscillations, since that is our belief. Since the heart is linked to such reactions, when someone is at peace with themselves, their heart is not overburdened but remains calm, and when overcome by emotions, the organ reacts accordingly.

The same cannot be said of the lungs, so medicine is just beginning to understand their self-regenerative ability. Of course, there may be other beliefs and habits that can temporarily affect this pair of organs in specific cases, such as smoking. However, for most of us, the lungs are unique, because humanity has strengthened their *regenerative* capacity through beliefs. Naturally, due to material conditions, a lack of oxygen will still lead to disincarnating; nonetheless, we trust so fully the act of breathing that it has strengthened our lungs and improved their capacity for self-regeneration. The same can be said for everything else. Whatever we trust, we strengthen.

Some people may say to us, "So repetitive, you keep going on and on about beliefs and choices." Our reply would be, "Is it not repetitive for humanity to keep reliving the same cycles for millennia, as history has taught? Is it not repetitive for spirits, over many reincarnations, to deliberately limit themselves to certain beliefs?" From the beginning, many masters have shown us that, in understanding that everything arises from our chosen beliefs, we free ourselves up to consciously create our experiences.

Gods. You are gods. We are gods. All of us, beings of all shapes and sizes, constituting everything that is, as parts of God. Some might mistake a statement like this with a superiority complex. Nevertheless, there is only one of us, nothing more and nothing less. Only the mind that thinks that way. Like it or not, believe it or not, we are gods. You can deny this and experience it otherwise, in the same way you can experience yourself in this plenitude. We have eternity to be and create ourselves. Do you really believe anything less is in store for you? Give it a try, what do you have to lose?

And so, we ask you, beyond your biological form, can anyone extinguish your life, once it is eternal? Can anyone give it to you? So, what is there to be afraid of?

# CHAPTER 18

M any authors, researchers, and mediums have already discussed and begun to explain life beyond what is known as death, both on earth and further away. Yes, there is life on several planes, both here and across multiple expanses of space. Although a wealth of evidence has already been left to us as a legacy by mediums like Francisco Cândido Xavier and researchers like Ian Stevenson, Jim B. Tucker, and Bruce Greyson, who made the first solid discoveries about reincarnation and near-death experiences, we affirm there is still much to come, from which new research and discoveries will be made. Such revelations will have an impact on human daily lives, providing signs of effective spiritual communications, which are, by the way, uninterrupted, though they frequently go unnoticed. Establish what you want to experience, of your own free will, opening yourself to the storehouse of spiritual information at your disposal, gathering the kind of content that works together with your experience. Although studying the literature and existing cases might be beneficial, the essential is living towards the blossoming of your spirituality in good faith, coherence, and sublimity.

Incarnation is a process of experimentation in conjunction with the means offered by a world under certain condition. Though beings disincarnate, they incarnate once again so they can experiment with different forms and not become attached to the patterns assimilated in a single lifetime. Thus, the spirit reaches new levels of refinement over time, facilitating its evolution. In the state experienced in this world (the Universe is home to matter in unimaginable states), matter creates a field of experience with relatively slow-moving events to provide adequate material for observation, assimilation, and the creation of baggage—all of which aid in the expansion of consciousness. It is through reincarnations that we have the opportunity not only to experience the cause and effect of our choices, but also to review and renew them.

In the case of beings who are no longer incarnate in this environment, that is, those who no longer need a physical medium of that nature, there are certain differences in the way events and experiences manifest. Nonetheless, laws are universal, albeit fluid. The planet we live on is made up of various fields of experience on more or less equivalent levels, with physical and spiritual counterparts, each corresponding dimension supporting the other.

The relationship of the body with the mind is analogous to the relationship of the Earth with the spiritual world, between its physical aspect and its subtle realm, which is nearly invisible from the material counterpart's perspective. The spiritual world is to planet Earth as thoughts are to the human brain. Spiritual reality is akin the reality people experience in their most vivid dreams. Rather than physical attributes, it consists of mental and emotional matter, managed with greater influence, dynamism, and perception by the disincarnate consciousness. For this reason, the realities of the spiritual world are maintained by the group's consciousness and their respective types of thought and energy. By the way, we might say that you have never left the Spiritual reality; you have only included a physical attachment for you to investigate in this existence, associating yourself with a perceptual state ideal for your spirit at this time.

The human beings' physical characteristics do not allow them to see ultraviolet or infrared light, nor hear ultrasound or infrasound frequencies. Beyond the limits of incarnate human senses (both to higher and lower frequencies) there is a range of information that moves *immensely* toward density and subtlety, far beyond the human's ability to perceive. The fact that something is invisible does not attest to its lack of existence, it only demonstrates our ignorance of its existence and it does not mean that this ignored fact does not have an influence on us.

Bacteria, viruses, and microscopic organisms usually go unseen, yet they constantly interact with other forms of life. As we gaze at the night sky, we cannot fathom or identify its vast immensity, drifting among stars and planets, which we merely see as space. Forces like magnetism, gravity, thoughts, gases, atoms, and countless other energetic forces belong to and make up this interactive Universe and are real whether we see them, understand them or not. Similarly, the spiritual dimension influences the world as much as any of these other examples, but with its own peculiarities, which human beings gradually grasp in their discoveries.

Just as in civilization there are different countries, states, and cities with dissimilar cultures, characteristics, and circumstances (certain locations experience constant war and conflict, while others live in admirable peace or relative respect), the same occurs among beings in the spiritual world, although more intensely. There are relationships on one side just as there are on the "other side," where everything originates and continues. There is a lot of activity in the spiritual spheres. The difference is that in Spirituality, spirits are grouped by the energy their choices promote. It is as if the truth were much closer to the surface and the chaff was separated from the wheat. The type of vibration generated by choices is what determines relationships, with less interference by physical circumstances. This is why there is a place for everything and everyone's proposals. However, a broader truth is that there are not two sides, but only different forms of the only energy there is.

Many people believe that Spirituality is far away, in a distant place, but it is everywhere, only on a different level. Just as there are places that are more or less populated by humanity, such as cities, forests, or deserts, the same happens on the subtle plane, in spiritual cities, havens and transit zones intensely altered by the consciousness involved. Oftentimes, when the frequencies are compatible, there will be simultaneous and parallel areas between the two dimensions. However, in the astral world—as it is also called, the subtle geographic structure may not be necessarily proportional to the physical world since they are not made up of the same material density. The regions are uniquely established and transitorily shaped by their inhabitants' vibrational frequency and sustained by the group consciousness—not by fixed locations or preconfigured zones like separate physical environments. These regions are constantly modified by the energy of everyone involved, similar to a shared dream.

Many disincarnate spirits are intimately connected to the lives of incarnate beings, for there are family members (in the sense of becoming family through closeness) going through various experiences who are watched and helped in their life purposes and choices. However, in certain situations, some spirits can become tired, such as on occasions where their work is to support multitudes of disincarnate beings, or when their family members are experiencing unnecessary hardship. At these times, spirits from other locations approach to help those who might feel exhausted, helping them to get back on their feet and renew themselves, according to their choices, so that these beings can resume the work to which they so completely devote themselves. Everywhere in the Universe, everyone, incarnate and disincarnate alike, is offered help, forming countless relationships among countless spirits and levels of experience, strengthened by love.

There are no hierarchies of importance and value, since everyone, incarnate and disincarnate, is a spirit, each in their own moment and set of choices. No one has been or ever will be more or less than anyone else. In the eyes of the soul, everyone is a being of the Universe. There are no outsiders, only natives of Life and God. Each person's home is where they are at any given time. The only "differentiation" is the one in which different choices and momentary beliefs develop among spirits, in accord with their energetic frequencies, which vary in time. Spirits do not necessarily measure time and space in seconds or hours, or physical distances; rather, it is their state of consciousness and their cultivated beliefs that tend to draw their experience of time and space. More expanded and subtle vibrations permeate incredible realities, which are maintained by beings who are closer to love and consciousness. Yet those who vibrate in intense mental and emotional confusion, confluent with disrespect and suffering, generally cling to addiction. These beings tend to maintain structures around them which correspond to those mechanisms, along with other individuals in similar circumstances. There is no heaven or hell aside from the internal states reflected in our experience.

Among the gifts of living life after life is the fact that we continue creating our experience, along with those we choose to share it with. This is a skill we never lose, wherever we are. We are creators. The set of beliefs and mainly the content of energy carried by each person is what influences their first experiences on the other side. There is no privilege or trickery since, unlike what many people believe, anyone who has created "hell" around themselves can change it at any time, insofar as they begin to make new choices. Unimaginable support and unconditional, ubiquitous, and indescribable love are offered each instant to individuals who experience the death of their physical body, and while such offers may go largely unnoticed, they can be used through each person's free choice.

Let us take a closer look at a few of these matters, through a simple explanation. Get ready. There is no empty space between the heavenly bodies in the Universe, since everything is energy. Nor is there physical matter in the form we see it with our eyes. Matter is a *virtual physical* reality. Certain areas of physics are getting closer to understanding this. Scientists have already disclosed that not even 1% of an atom is made up of matter, just a tiny nucleus and miniscule electrons. In other words, practically the entire atom is apparently empty. Approximately 99.9% of atoms are estimated to be just space. Yes, 99.9%. That alone is a good reason to change many paradigms of the human mind. Amazingly, these atoms still make up cells, arrange bodies, make up the structure of land and are what heavenly bodies are made of, after all, they are the known elements of the Universe so far. Your body, apparently solid, loses definition at the atomic level. Therefore, practically everything is made of "empty" space. The deeper scientists look at matter, the more they see it as disappearing to the point where some believe it to be empty. Therefore, instead of "empty", a term like "formless space" becomes more appropriate (with a double-meaning: space without form, and space from which pure information arises). In that indeterminate space, all electrons and energy operate as *infinite possibilities and relationships,* a field where information can become organized in different forms.

In fact, nothing is completely empty, only formless space abound with possibilities that have yet to be defined, as opposed to those that have been defined. For that reason, in those areas supposedly absent of anything, where some believed there was merely nothing, pulses the energy that holds up the structure of the Universe, immanent sources originating from the Absolute. The Absolute source, stardust, arises in minimal components in every corner of the Universe, so that each miniscule part only remains active according to what is compatible with its moment.

Let us go further. Imagine the following: we know that the Universe is expanding and that everything is in motion. We not only know that space moves as one, but that structures of "empty" space surrounding the celestial bodies (planets, stars etc.) are also in motion, operating as a kind of space-time fabric. In order for the cosmos to continue expanding, this formless space should also expand and change. For the planets to orbit around the sun and stars—and continue the same locomotor process among themselves—the space around those structures moves dynamically, curving and bending to cause the effect of planets moving around their stars. This effect became known as gravity, brought about by the movement of that "empty" space between materials, provoking attractions, and the movement of information between space/time.

How would empty space in a vacuum bend itself or move? Obviously, if it were empty, as nothingness, it would not move. Therefore, there is no empty space, only invisible space (empty of matter visible at this frequency) in a different state. For the "network" of formless space to move and readjust itself (for example, in the region where planet Earth rotates around the Sun), there must be another "parallel space behind" (or "within"), supporting that locomotion, like interposed, correlated extensions that allow those movements to be carried out. That other space is what is called another reality, dimension, level, or plane. The dimensions overlap each other and are everywhere, not as something separate, but as interconnected realities, like frequencies that have different vibrations. In fact, there is no such thing as dimensions. There is only one thing in reality. Dimensions are perceptions created by our minds, products of our perspective and our senses, although they may be useful for understanding. Formless space is filled with energy in a different form than the physical matter. There is matter on other dimensions, it is just structured differently and vibrates at a different frequency than physical matter. It is as simple as human ears not being able to hear sounds that dogs can, or unable to see colors that certain birds see.

Imagine, *symbolically*, that the known physical reality in this world is like a computer programming written according to this experimental reality. While there are other realities in different dimensions, they are incompatible with this computer's programming. This is why we have not been able to find solid particles to prove the existence of other planes, since their matter (form) is configured differently. Currently, the only way to research and learn about them is through indirect, non-physical mechanisms of cause and effect, which indicate interdimensional relationships, such as near-death experiences, mediumship and interactions with the formless space, bringing about new logical possibilities.

For millennia, throughout the history of our current civilization, especially in western culture, people had a narrow view of the workings of the human body. Some eastern cultures, through Acupuncture, Ayurveda, and other ancient and spiritually-based medicines, opened themselves to knowledge that allowed them to provide effective assistance to human beings. However, global society has experienced long periods of miscomprehension, ignorance and mockery that have prevented improvements and renovations in our understanding of life. It took a long time for human beings to understand physiological functions, organs, viscera, diseases, and anatomy in general, which had complex consequences in their lives.

Those who ventured to make these discoveries, through scientific research or healing work, were subjected to great prejudice for more than a dozen centuries. Many people have been persecuted, tortured, and killed just for trying to demonstrate yet-to-be-seen truths and transcend conventions by improving human lives. As an example, the first doctors who suggested the importance of thorough hand-washing before performing surgery were ridiculed. Epidemics, lack of basic sanitation, and individual illnesses were not understood, and few people knew how to deal with them. The lack of knowledge led to mistaken procedures like unnecessary amputations, which were all too common. Before the gradual emergence of new knowledge, treatments, and technology, billions of people suffered, became ill and died due to the human arrogance and lack of skills to deal with new developments. Recently, although there are still many apparently forsaken people around the world, individual and public health, as well as the possibility of curing many diseases are more well known and frequently worked on in civilization's daily life.

Currently, mediumship, psychic, and spiritual abilities are other fields that humans can explore. When they come to be well understood, studied, and practiced, they will allow human beings to transcend the suffering and illusions that now accost humanity. All over the world, cases of schizophrenia and other mental disturbances are directly linked to imbalance and improper use of these human abilities. Instead of being seen as incurable diseases, they can be honed to become incredibly functional tools. More subtle cases within familial, romantic, and social relationships are also as common as they are unnoticed. Sensitivity disorders in varying degrees are more common than flu amid the world population. The field of personal sensitivity refinement and of humanity as a whole is an exceptional advancement of the human being—the refinement of the conscious use of energy moved by the spirit, from the emotions to the mind. There is nothing supernatural in this little understood and researched science. On the contrary, these are abilities that operate according to entirely natural laws, as unknown as the human body itself once was.

Mediumship has become known by intercommunication with spirits; however, as the name says, it is not only medium for disincarnated spirits, but it is the ability to intermediate any energy, according to its dynamics. Mediumship and sensitivity can be compared to the electrical wiring of a house. A person who is unfamiliar with their own psychic structures, and unskilled at dealing with them, is like a house with a powerful electrical system without a breaker box, outlets, or on/off switches, inducing electrical hazards. Due to the loose and sometimes bare wires, the electrical wiring can be triggered accidentally, leading to a system breakdown and electrical discharges that shock residents or visitors. While we all know the dangers of a poorly-wired house, we are just now catching our first glimpses of the imbalances that occur in our own bodies. By learning how to better deal with our energetic circuits, we will be sure to install the proper "switches" in the consciousness of our inner home to respond effectively to our daily interactions, thus enabling a more wholesome, fruitful, invigorating coexistence.

Returning to the previous example, and just to illustrate, if the reality in each dimension is like a type of computer configured a certain way, let us suppose that each of us is like a program in that computer, such as a game or file. For us to run properly on another operating system, in other words, for us to exist consciously in another dimension, we must program ourselves for that new reality. Every reality, in every dimension is virtual, because no reality is absolute. Each level is only relative to its own virtual reality, although some encompass others amidst the Absolute (whatever is projected onto those virtual realities). Each reality is a reflection of the Absolute, supported by all the different types of consciousness and perceptions that are its composition. We are all like spiritual programs in the computer of eternal life, and we can transform these programs by getting to know ourselves.

The spirit is beyond all virtual realities; in other words, it never dies, and communicates with different levels, often without the current physical mechanism's awareness. The body temporarily houses the programming for this physical system of life. In order to switch computers (dimensional realities), you must change your programming, much like a file that receives an update to operate on a new computer. From another perspective, this is what some people call "Enlightenment," which, through expanded consciousness, is nothing more than a spiritual process of internal changes of vibrational frequency (modification of your program's structure).

Death, or disincarnation, is when the process of changing frequency occurs from a predominantly *extrinsic* cause, in other words, disincarnation by physical circumstances, leading to body failure. In this case, there is a temporary dimension "switch" in order to renew and adapt oneself to the programming of the next physical body in a process known as reincarnation. In another situation, there are states of enlightenment in which the switch in frequency occurs from a predominantly *intrinsic* cause. In other words, the spirit no longer intends to program itself at this physical level, and begins to program itself in a subtler vibration, or, better said, in a new, broader virtual reality system.

According to this clarifying metaphor, mediumship and sensitivity are like the Internet, allowing some contact among different computational systems and making information sharing possible. Depending on how one uses the "Internet," this marvelous unifying tool can become a means of propagating increasingly universal truths. In that sense, Spirituality intensively manages this connection, seeking to assist and collaborate on aspects previously established by spirits as well as on constant changes in everyday choices. Through this network, information is improved upon, consciousness expansion processes are initiated, and cause-effect relationships are clarified, for the simple reason that disincarnate spirits have already experienced life as the incarnates have, but currently have a broader view of eternity, besides the fact that we are all a universal family.

Each person on Earth is surrounded by various spiritual companions, one after the other over time. If people were fully aware of these commonplace relationships, they would be distracted from their everyday tasks. For this and other reasons, there are certain limits to perceptual communication between the levels, since even people with exceptional mediumship never see everything. The more they see, the more they realize how little is seen. The energetic movement brought forth by their choices fosters closeness between beings. Those who seek a sincere path of self-knowledge and assistance, according to their purposes, are helped by these beings; the truer the purpose of their actions, the stronger the spiritual support. In the same way, criminals, for example, are accompanied in their temporary intentions by beings who have the same propensity for such thoughts, emotions, and attitudes, and who help them in whatever activities they have decided to embark upon. These different dimensions inevitably relate to each other, since everything in the Universe *multiplies* when there is a gathering of similar intentions.

It is still unimaginable for many to understand the movement generated by Spirituality in assisting humanity, from the smallest to the largest groups of people and living beings. There is great amount of knowledge and work to be done available in the spiritual world, since no information is lacking in the Universe of God. This is because spirits remember many of their previous experiences on both levels, while incarnate beings do not remember most of their spiritual baggage, so that they may reformulate it gradually.

Spirituality observing human experience is like a group of individuals engaged in watching a movie, one that, nevertheless, has multiple alternative sequences, although the end may be the same. When watching the film from various angles, it is possible to verify the various changes that can happen and understand which has the greatest propensity to manifest itself. What would it be like if you could contact some of the characters in the story and help them? From this angle, the movie is like a single episode in a series, in which the main character is so identified with the role that they forget what exactly happened in prior episodes, even though those events have influenced the current episode. By the same token, the characters do not fully understand the objectives and sequence of the series. Nevertheless, the group of individuals watching the series, because they have the prerogative to interact, fully comprehends the experience of the characters involved. The spirits watch over the plot and, when possible, interact with the protagonist, thus contributing to the making of a better movie. This is Spirituality's perspective, different from that of human beings. Human beings are similar to the characters in a series, playing out the script, which is constantly being written and rewritten by all the beings involved. Meanwhile, behind the scenes, their companions in the spiritual world act like a production crew, perfecting the filmmaking process in such a way that, in the end, the director is Life.

Generally, all assistance is based on the law of best use, since Spirituality works on the principle that nothing is lost, everything is transformed. Who can accurately say that a given experience was not worthwhile for the spirit? Therefore, we can undoubtedly say that everything can be made use of, as well as transformed. The Universe respects all choices and objectives of the beings. That is the reason there are so many people who find themselves out of balance and unaware of their conditions, but who still manage to contribute as channels of assistance whenever possible, even in their daily lives. If spiritual work were based on each person's exact judgment, almost nothing could be done, which is why there is no reason to judge anyone, rather, just contribute to everyone's improvement as much as they are open to it, making the most of the possibilities with increasing mastery.

In every realm, there are no experiences that beings cannot utilize. All of those who think they are experiencing sad lives—horrific moments or cruelties practiced against them, their spirit will certainly make the most of those experiences; they can be of service in other ways, under revisited approaches. Nothing is in vain. The principle known in science by Lavoisier's law, that nothing is lost or created from nothing, that everything is transformed and can be used is a foundation of the Universe that flows on all levels, from the physical to the spiritual.

Each action, in each of your existences, will remain with you eternally. Spirit carries the memory of all knowledge acquired, of each and every hour. Although understanding this might be maddening for some, there is nothing to fear. It is precisely for this reason that temporary forgetfulness is the divine opportunity for renovation available to everyone who needs it. Even though no memory can be entirely removed from any spirit, nor can spirit permanently lose or erase it, at every moment and before the truth of eternal life there exists the possibility of complete renewal, spanning all time. The core of this question lies, magnificently, in the opportunity that, in due time, there is always the possibility of bringing light to any time span of the spirit, dark or dazzling, reviving the experience and renewing that window of time—like the mythological phoenix *reborn* from its own ashes, taking off again on a new flight.

Every thought reaches eternity. That is a strong statement, but it is true. Nevertheless, although a chosen thought vibrates with its unending presence, change is the indelible law of this Universe that enables levels of thoughts to expand, embracing those obsolete in a more eminent and loving form. A mark in spiritual time is consolidated by the *choice* of only a single thought or event, which remains suspended in time, similar to a loose or incomplete part of a toy, waiting for the rest of the parts to be added, which will modify the way it is seen. Although it is eternal and present, any mark can be transformed in this very moment as the toy is completed with the other parts. Finally, it will no longer be a seemingly useless loose part, having transformed itself into a "ready-to-play-with toy," fulfilling the objectives of the spirit in the live game, through consciousness.

Everyone carries their spirit's objectives along with them, to be carried out at the given existential moment. Most times, these are unknown by the conscious mind, briefly perceived in the midst of the synchronicity of life. These designs are a personal matter; the constant transformation of the being as it comes closer to God through life experiences. Although these objectives may be personal, they are connected to intents that are somewhat similar, forming the framework of experiences in everybody's lives, revealing them in their joint journeys. At the same time, they are assisted by those who, through their wisdom of universal interactivity, are brought with the right conditions for those encounters.

Oftentimes, comprehending and taking responsibility for the "package," or the whole of your current incarnation—which is always determined by your own spirit—helps you in your experience, by aligning yourself with your being's purposes. From experience to experience, every spirit has an array of aspects to work on to expand its consciousness, which is why human beings are designed as multifactorial, multi-dimensional beings. There are as many facets of oneself to be known, explored, and renewed by love as there are stars in the sky. These unique features of your being are brought to the surface one by one over time, naturally, as ever-present opportunities to expand your consciousness.

Before reincarnation, the spirit determines the nature of its choices, deciding beforehand which aspects it wants to work on and will seek to experience and attracting them. Still, it does not define all the specific ways this will happen, as these will be determined or altered by free choices in everyday life. A human being's subconscious mind is structured beforehand by the spirit, so that, as it receives information from the world since birth, it will store, distribute, and organize it according to the flows of its objectives, forming them in their experience. Nevertheless, certain groups of learned concepts and customs can complicate and delay the expression of spiritual purposes, because of tendencies, but will never fail the being during reincarnations. Although we never lose the freedom to believe that they have failed us and experience them this way. Realities are also created from states of unconsciousness. In the same way, one can favor the establishment of spiritual objectives. The more conscious we are of the previously subconscious content that emerges at each right time, from the depths of our minds, the more we will be able to transform it and create our reality.

Within the laws of physics, if an astronaut were to travel through space, approaching stars, spheres, and different kinds of matter on their journey, they would come back to meet humans on Earth, after having experienced the intensity of time differently than those who had remained on the planet. Even biological parents could return physically younger than their children. Can you even conceive something like that? Just imagine spirits, who are neither ruled by material experience nor physical time, but by the amplitude and reach of their spiritual experience. This is why everything in the material plane originates from the spiritual plane, where time is incomparably more comprehensive.

In the everyday physical world, human beings experience the environment as something well-defined and apparently stable. They need a space to work in, a house to hold their belongings and protect them from the elements—from cold or heat, rain, or shine—to keep them from being constantly exposed. They need to move from one place to another in buses or cars within the limits of space and time that apparently hold steady. In Spirituality, under different material conditions, beings move more easily than incarnate beings, having stripped off the physical body that they used temporarily. They currently enjoy a fluid body, so that they are no longer subject to the laws of the earthly environment. As soon as humanity opens itself to its spiritual nature, such principles will increasingly reveal themselves to everyone's comprehension.

Although there is constant assistance and communication between the planes, nobody belongs exclusively to anyone. All beings, incarnate and disincarnate alike, are free and participants in universal evolution. Angels, guides, or spiritual mentors (as some tend to call them) do not belong to anyone but are still companions on the beautiful journey of eternal life. These spiritual friends and collaborators work towards the objectives of both beings—just like parents who guide and help their children, but who have also received help from others and still do. We give and receive help, comprising an infinite universal relationship of interaction, sharing, and mutual assistance.

In this connection, because disincarnate spirits move on a subtler level, they approach humans through thoughts and emotions. A person's emotional reactions are like cracks that open in a field around them, allowing for approaches in agreement with the content of those feelings. Imbalanced emotions like fear, anger, pride, possessiveness, vanity, or envy attract company with those characteristics, while those that are harmonious and outstanding in their love attract presences with these features. Many more forces of the Universe move around and through you than you usually perceive. The same is true for all of us. Although it can be done this way, it is not necessarily through specific evocations or rituals that we commune with spiritual company that harmoniously shares our intentions. Another way is through the full presence of your being, mental observation, and genuine feelings as you make your own choices, perhaps making it possible to spread love to your neighbors. Prayer, when it transcends words, comes from within and is carried out in the sincere expression of intention and transformation of feelings, always turns into bliss. Prayer is not about God's need to know what is happening inside someone, because even before someone expresses it, Life already knows what is inside each of us; rather, prayer is an opportunity for your being to know and express what it is choosing, as it connects with all that is. Every word spoken is a prayer, an affirmation of Life of what we are doing with our freedom. The remarkable beauty of eternity, in its multiple interactions that forge deep and unique ties between beings, is supported by the principle that energy is Life and every feeling is an intense energy generator, the beautiful force we feel arise within us.

# CHAPTER 19

C ertain civilizations and peoples from every corner of the world have had well-developed customs regarding the power of dreaming. Every time they woke up after a night of sleep, tribe members would get together so they could share their dreams and perceptions, revealing profound mysteries of consciousness and spiritual relationships. Many tribes were very close to the spiritual world and often received information about processes of consciousness and how to improve their lives; including knowledge about medicinal plants and natural elements. In this way, some ideas about the art of dreaming were passed on from generation to generation. Certainly, this still occurs among individuals who cultivate a common purpose, affinity, trust, and considerable compatibility among each other, leading to this type of sharing. The dream experience is part of the human content in every period, even today. Who among us has never gone to bed having our head full of questions or aspirations, and woken up the following day with the answers we needed?

Dreams are arranged in multiple ways. We will now discuss some of their basic features. When approached from the *time* perspective, they tend to take place in one of the following ways. The first is a recollection of the past, either from your current life or a previous one. It occurs when former experiences have left a profound mark on the spirit and may even be affecting you currently. Another way is when dreams bring awareness of something that may occur in the future. This kind of dream can show a tendency of what might happen, where you are headed unless you change course by making a new choice. These two types of dreams are less common than our habitual ones. Finally, the most common dreams are related to our life's current circumstances. They reflect on aspects and patterns that are currently interfering in your life. Nevertheless, looking closer we will see that everything affecting our lives, whether considered part of our past or future, is in its own way part of our present.

Dreams can also present themselves in different forms when seen from the *configuration* angle. The first one we will mention is that the human mind is full of concepts, words, images, symbols, sounds, and assemblies that allow it to form representations, reusing previously-captured information. Nevertheless, different peoples and cultures attribute different meanings to images, symbols, and words, which means they can create different ideas about what is seen during the dream. Some characteristics are fundamental enough to be universal, but the symbols resulting from dreams are directly related to their attributed meanings, both individually and collectively regarding where they are inserted.

Sometimes, a dream can occur so that all its characters and elements work as a reflection of the person dreaming, as parts of their "I," in which each composition appearing to them is representing something occurring in themselves. Occasionally, they can show something perceived about other people, or occurrences affecting their lives, also attributing symbols to those figures. All representations we view in our dreams—though they often do not make sense to the intellectual mind—pertain to deep work by way of patterns and types of energy that shape aspects of our consciousness, freely using symbols as means to create connections. Because of its many images, this is the type of dreaming most normally recognized by people, at least superficially. However, such figures cannot always be interpreted literally; rather it is the energy behind the forms that reveals their true meaning through feeling. This is because the mind uses the images it has on hand in the subconscious level, as a façade for its work on a set of sensations, energies, and feelings. This kind of dreaming is a message that emerges from the depths of the mind, allowing it to become conscious. Still, the mind does not need to understand every detail in a dream for it to influence the state of the experience because when something happens in a dream, it is guarded away deep in the mind to reemerge at the right time.

Another configuration of dreaming that happens more sporadically is one that, instead of making use of symbols from the individual's mind, is composed of information—words, images, sounds, or other types of content—previously unknown to the incarnate mind. It has now become available to our being through a well-tuned spiritual contact or a connection to a collective field.

For its part, the third dream configuration we will talk about is extremely common but often goes unnoticed because it is apparently abstract. With no representations, images or symbols of any kind, these dreams are characterized by intense sensations of energetic movements, independent of form, that stir up feelings and free information, like direct knowledge about something we have not put into words yet.

Finally, when seen from the *purpose* angle, dreams are here presented in two different ways. The first purpose of dreaming is to energetically prepare your being for occurrences happening soon after you wake up, as well as for later, sometimes even months or years later. Certain energies interact and organize themselves, including those of everyone involved in a context. Countless people go to sleep feeling there is no solution to their disagreements with someone else, only to find as they wake up that both sides have either resolved the disagreements or that they have gotten worse. As we dream, our relationships of all kinds may not be occurring physically, but on a subtler plane where emotions and mental paths flow, our relationships continue uninterruptedly, also foreseeing affinities or hostilities that may occur later. Occasionally, people involved in a certain context will share their dreams, finding that at times, their dreams complement each other. Sleeping is the body's way of resting by turning off physical perceptions, while the spirit, mind and feelings reorganize themselves and work more freely, redirecting and creating new experiences while the body sleep.

The second purpose of dreaming is when your consciousness interacts on the spirit level with beings living on other planes while your body sleeps, reconnecting you with your spiritual nature, as well as allowing guidance and clarifications. Closely related individuals that have disincarnated, beings known during other existences, as well as friends, mentors, and beings from your spiritual family, relate to each person with a frequency that few imagine possible. Practically every time we sleep, we interact with the consciousness of beings who are no longer incarnate, as well as some who are, through *spiritual unfoldment*. However, for most people this occurs on a level tending towards unconsciousness, while others have a greater or lesser degree of awareness of their relationships in the spiritual world.

Someone might ask, "How can I recognize the nature of a dream?" "Are they past lives or future possibilities?" "Are they representations of my own 'I,' perceptions of an event or someone else?" Observation of dream characteristics, especially the sensations, energies, and feelings that they produce in us—when we do not apply our judgments or assumptions and let ourselves enter that sphere with the proper attention, will, on their own, reveal their nature through experience and feeling. As we consider our dream experiences, an indispensable part of the human experience, we recognize our ability to feel and identify their energy and purposes. We discover that lucid dreaming is possible. Still, even when we do not clearly remember what happened during an unfoldment, this is not a problem, because the information is stored at a deep and hidden level of the mind until it spontaneously manifests itself during experiences. Frequently, in our daily lives, we may think a piece of insight or awareness came to us out of nowhere, when all the consciousness involved actually worked for a long time before an insight became known to us at the present time.

Spiritual unfoldment, out-of-body or extracorporeal experience, is the consciousness' ability to leave the body and move through other levels beyond matter, either while your body is awake or asleep. Therefore, it is not the physical body that unfolds, but one or more links of consciousness are extended to locations related at the frequency flowing according to our choices, made at all times, day and night. In fact, every thought emitted about a certain environment, or someone moves toward its destination to a greater or lesser degree of intensity as unfoldment begins. Some people acquire the ability to unfold themselves somewhat consciously and can perceive and move their emotional, mental, and spiritual interactions on other levels, as well as, to a certain degree, take note of and understand those of other individuals, always in resonance with the energy they send out.

The mind is a creative system in motion, like a gear system. Each thought is directly linked to a gear in the mental setup. More frequent thoughts are represented by more gears. These structures, composed and shaped by the set of beliefs and thoughts we nourish every day, promote the creation of our experience in the world. Our mental system is always operating as a large power generator, directing the way this abundant power will be used. Therefore, the way we think is directly proportional to the energy moved by our mental generator, promoting part of our expression in the world. With discordant thoughts, the gears stop turning together and can lead to chaos in the system, such as with cases of doubt, indecision, or discord. Our mental generator, far more perfect than any machine, has a natural way of operating, available due to being in balance with our being, where our gears/thoughts flow harmoniously in constructive movement.

As we sleep, our mind and brain tend to organize themselves spontaneously, so the "gears" can fit together more in accordance with the aims of our experience. Meditation, by stopping the mind's internal dialogue or observing it clearly, also produces these beneficial effects for our being while we are awake. By allowing ourselves to meditate and observe ourselves a few moments during the day, active information begins to organize itself more clearly, even more so when we consciously enter these states naturally on any occasion.

Nevertheless, most of the human mind's content is still filled and reinforced by numerous illusions. Daily experience produces a smokescreen that can obscure our awareness and any possibility for clarity, bringing our still existing tendencies to the surface. Very strong are the human tendencies triggered by influences emerging from experiences. Frequently, human perception is obscured by fog, surrounded by curtains that prevent many other energies from flowing. Only through great love, self-discipline, and firmness in our life choices can we avoid succumbing to these designs, opening ourselves to a consistent presence that transforms everything.

In our current world, which is based on a variety of technologies, we might notice that as we make repeated searches about certain subjects on a virtual platform like the Internet, these topics will begin to appear more frequently in research suggestions, icons, and corresponding advertisements, until eventually becoming automated in the system's memory. They are often called personalized data. The same is true for how our minds operate. Repeatedly choosing certain thoughts causes automation of mental behaviors. Along these lines, we can also observe that the use of these technologies also suggests this principle. Today, we see countless children, teenagers, and grownups taken by the illusion that they are using virtual tools when often exactly the opposite is true. Fixated on the possibility of virtually promoting themselves as someone they are not but want to appear to be (because very few people still use these tools in an instructive and advantageous way for all), we frequently see people deluded by automation, as much by this mental behavior as by the technology they believe they are using. It can be proven by looking at the numerous folks who will even interrupt their sleep—their body's time to rest because they feel a need to answer messages immediately, updates, or online comments. In such cases, relationships, postponed and disregarded in real everyday life, are sought in illusory means, in daily attempts to get away, in which many are content to fulfill their needs on these platforms, building isolation in their inner solitude. As a natural consequence, habits originating like this lead to tough consequences for the consciousness. Still, we should remember that with all tendencies or possibilities new choices and results are always available, meaning transformation can be immediate. Touching on this subject is worthwhile since many people born into new generations are faced with a world full of these characteristics. In such a case, they can also receive, to a greater degree, the opportunity for benevolent instruction. In some cases, these technological instruments can be found even in places where there is not enough food or water for some inhabitants. The proposal has become so common as to disseminate itself, however, if it were reconstructed in the truth of love, we would come to use these technologies as tools and vehicles of dissemination for a society regenerated through harmonization.

Loneliness is one of the greatest illusions ever carried in the human heart. Essentially, what we call solitude does not exist. Isolation occurs in experience only when the belief in solitude exists, because a state of loneliness is only created by the beliefs creating its experience. What are those beliefs? The first is the belief that we are separate. But neither does what we call separation exist, except at the level of appearances. We are made of unity since everything is entirely related. Therefore, the illusion can be overcome through the wisdom emanating from every living being.

Belief in separation has become a widespread part of the human experience, producing a variety of subsequent illusions. The state of loneliness many people feel, if we observe it closely, is based on the idea that there is something one can be isolated from, as in the idea that being in a physical environment without other human beings around means being alone. However, we are never alone. One of the greatest illusions emerging from this process is that a person's thoughts are isolated from the rest. Beings can become aware that although they may not be close to other people in physical bodies, they are relating with them on other levels. Every thought about something or someone reaches its destination immediately. There is a level where we all know what others think or feel, although we may not have this kind of awareness yet. Thus, every thought we have about someone is a subtle conversation with that person.

By the same token, the level of the feeling is shared immediately and at any physical distance, depending on its depth. Likewise, not only are we surrounded by the energy of Life, it is immanently part of every one of us. Much of the feelings and thoughts people cultivate when addressing other people, are also communicated directly to other aspects of Life, which has been and always will be with and in us. Who has never complained about a day, or offered thanks for one? Who has never felt cozy next to a fire or purified by the touch of water? Who has never felt embraced by the trees? In its own way, Life talks to us, giving and receiving each expression. Let us not forget spiritual company as well, which is there while we sleep or in the subtleties of our intuition. Solitude is a mental illusion and can be treated as such, so we can transcend it and experience a state of union.

If we watch what happens when someone feels connected to others, we will understand some of the characteristics of union. When you feel connected to someone, you first sense their presence. There is someone else with you. Next, you consider what you want and what they want at that moment. In other words, you intuitively look for a way to become closer, to share the present moment, either out of fear or love. Later, a space arises that allows for depth, where you learn a little more about the other person, and vice versa.

Still, what happens with those who find themselves with no one around? How do you feel when no one is close by? We say that the more we transcend the illusion, the less we feel alone because there is always a feeling of connection with everything, which in fact was always the case. We no longer crave physical presence as if it were a necessary condition; rather, we consider every opportunity the present moment gives us. In communion with the all, we can experience depth with Life, which we have come to know better, while it knows itself through us since connection is the nature of our being, of the state of union, we are all one.

In the arch of life, with its sumptuous portal, all incarnate brothers and sisters meet each other. They do not see it since it is invisible. They do not touch it since it is hidden. Nevertheless, this living portal, omnipresent and immaterial, still unceasingly opens itself before each unique spirit. Like someone who wakes up bothered by the daylight, preferring to return to darkened environments in an attempt at self-protection, do we fear facing the light, such is the luminosity emanating from the All? Or shall we open the living portal, so our spirit's carriage can pass through and along the streets of the mind as benevolent passages? To which mental conduct of the mind do we choose to give our attention? Fear is the greatest of illusions. However, Life completely respects every illusion as a way for truth to be revealed. May we have wisdom first. Eyes are the vehicles of the soul. Do they not shine as living proof? May we allow our eyes to become accustomed to the light with the same firmness that our feet touch the ground. With our vision enchanted by Love and Purpose, we will see the gift of Life, which gave us shadows to illuminate.

# CHAPTER 20

A person can tell us something our mind has yet to learn, something we may not know, but nonetheless, everything we hear is already known on a level beyond the mind. The spirit imbibes all the information of eternal life from the soul, finding this information in a whole and silent space available to every individual who achieves a state of presence, accessing innate and divine wisdom.

A wise person lives in a way that when they learn, they do it as if they know nothing; when they act, they act as if they know everything. This way, they learn everything and act in nothingness. Learning as if they do not know anything does not mean cultivating ignorance, but humility. Acting as if they know everything is not a sign of blind arrogance; it means they have confidence in the process. Nevertheless, knowing that they always learn while they act and act while they learn, a wise person realizes that they know everything and nothing at the same time.

All this wordplay arises because we are reaching the threshold of consciousness, the "line" separating mental knowledge from spiritual wisdom. There is a considerable difference between knowledge and wisdom. The mind does not know things, it knows about things. Spiritual wisdom, consequently, is direct knowledge about things through the spirit's experience, rather than a mere accumulation of concepts and ideas.

There are cases where the acquisition of more knowledge makes it difficult to remain humble. Sometimes, when we think we see a lot, we become blind, and sometimes we think we hear too well, we become deaf. There are happiness when we perceive the landscape surrounding us without considering it to be the only one, remembering there is an infinite unknown just beyond the horizon. In the same way, by listening to music without judging what we hear, we remain mindful of the eternal song.

Many of us think we are so knowledgeable that when we come into contact with words that instigate applied wisdom, we underappreciate, deride, and even ignore them, claiming that things are different in practice. However, what is true cannot be threatened; what is essential cannot be made extinct. It does not take long for experience to show its depth to each living being. Even if we reject the consciousness of love by considering it a false rumor, through our own experience, we will feel the actuality of its principles when they knock at our door, and we decide to open it.

We can learn about the process of building a house, studying masonry, framing, and how to arrange all the details to build a dwelling. It is not unlike learning about Life's laws, the principles of the spirit, and the logic behind the excellence of love. Still, are we the ones building the house of Life? In residential construction, the architect is the basis of knowledge about building, while the contractor is the one who applies direct knowledge. Both are hired to do what is needed to erect the home. However, in our spiritual lives, there is no way for us to hire someone else to apply wisdom. Although we can remind each other and collaborate as the architects and contractors in our lives, everyone is responsible for integrating their knowledge about things with applied spiritual wisdom, so the two can walk hand in hand. Self-discipline is the wisdom that fosters knowledge and action as one. Some of us truly apply living wisdom as a natural state amid simplicity, often without knowing how we do it, while others are overcrowded with concepts, ideas, and complex thoughts, and confused amid the seductions of the mental rhythm when the moment to be and act arrives. Those who unconditionally love know what those who merely know a lot have yet to understand. We are fortunate when we balance both qualities, of thought and action, revealing our being's conscious integrity.

All knowledge acquired is worthwhile when truly effective, assisting in the processes of spirit. Nevertheless, merely accumulating more information, though it may ennoble our social or professional daily lives, is of little use for our consciousness' effective travel in spiritual time. Whether it is fascination with an excessive quantity of concepts, or when a less skilled intellect stumbles over more complex ideas, when there is no legitimate spiritual purpose in the here and now, the mind takes the reins of experience and runs wild, while the spirit waits respectfully. One of the most unconscious forms of human communication is when two or more people struggle to single-mindedly convince each other of their point of view, without listening to anything aside from their own concepts and digressions. The nature of love will bring us closer to the truth, so that when communicating with our neighbors, through sincere and attentive listening and speaking, we naturally inspire each other to express ourselves in our own process and genuine path.

As we learn about things by intellect alone, abdicating our feeling, we might think that we know, when, actually, we only know that someone knows. Although knowing about other people's experiences is both fundamental and stimulating, such as when we are inspired by the paths of Jesus, Buddha, and other beings, consciously discerning the state of our own being at the moment is crucial, so that we may live the experience. Both those who yearn to accumulate more information and those who are inspired by the journeys of other masters are blessed when they support themselves with genuine intention, determining their choice steadfastly and applying it on their own path.

As long as we want to be great, more, or better, we will be excluding a part of ourselves, the other side of the coin. Desiring only greatness, or to be greater than someone else, attests to our limitations. Greatness is not composed solely of greatness; in order for it to be truly abundant and whole, it is composed first of littleness. Only through littleness do we find it; we discover integrity with some humility. For us to reach the higher steps of a staircase, we must start by climbing the first steps, lest we create illusions for ourselves by aiming too high without wanting to take the first steps. "Greatness" through pride bears illusory results, while true greatness sprouts in the field of littleness.

For a coin to be what it is, it is minted with two sides. One side states the value, and the other tells you where it has value. Manifestations of inner worth are similar. Our greatness is the coin's value side, while smallness is the base from which our manifestation has value and arises. Actually, the coin has more than two sides, but for it to work, it is but one in action. Life, even more so, is a coin of infinite sides.

Could there be anything greater than the Universe? The radiant All is composed of nothing less than countless small parts. Does not the cosmos create both the modest ladybug and the myriad of stars? Thus, proportions vanish since there is no way to measure or fit them into a defined model. Dimensions are lost, they are relative, leaving behind suffocating fixed limits. From atom to ocean, ocean to Earth, Earth to Sun, Sun to galaxy, and so on, proportionality is lost, the idea of what is supposedly big or small disappears, to emerge all that is. Are you big or small? Why not a Universe?

If a single human being can acquire wisdom as they age, imagine the wisdom acquired by Life itself over billions of years of evolution; in fact, that living wisdom is manifest in the Universe's every condition, as it is through a human being. A wise person has the essence of a child but is conscious as they exercise their nature. Children, before receiving various external influences, are completely connected to the present. They might cry, but, if the situation changes their tears can spontaneously be replaced by laughter. A wise person is true to themselves just like a child; however, they use their spirit's wisdom to deal consciously with their experience of the world.

The wise person's door is open to the spirit, and they act in accordance with their inner state. Therefore, they do not react in accordance with whatever situations or people try to impose on them. Instead, they naturally dissolve them by turning to the truth, without feeding into a vicious cycle. If someone insults them, they do not take it personally, feeling insulted and desiring revenge. They just keep being who they chose to be. If they choose to take a position, it will not be in keeping with the energy of the insult, but in accordance with whom they have chosen to be.

Our energetic presence is similar to a grid. When cleared up by the spirit, we have a peacefully open energy net. When external information comes as an insult, it will go through the net just like water. In other words, we recognize the insult, we are aware of it, but we do not hold on to it or react to it in the same way.

Continuing with our reference to the grid: when we do not use our innate wisdom, we experience a different result. These days, not dealing well with several emotional aspects is common to the human condition, until this type of occurrence is no longer necessary. When that is the case, we identify with the insult. Consequently, there are strict mental limits in our energetic grid that close things off as blocking areas, so that instead of allowing information to circulate freely through open spaces, it runs into barriers. Wherever there are contracted, closed off points in the energetic field, a type of receptacle is created where we gather and hold onto external information; either that or we ricochet it back to where it came from, often directing it at someone else. Either we swallow the insult, or we return it, maintaining the cycle. The same generally occurs with sensitivity. Love and wisdom liberate the flow of our energetic field, while fear blocks it.

Fear can give us a nearly undeniable need for protection. People attack each other by words, thoughts, distorted emotions, and even physical violence. Every need for defense attracts some type of compatible attack, just as every attack arises from the idea of preemptive defense. On a certain level, an attack is a request for assistance. Deep down, the person who attacks has a nagging fear, whatever form that might take. If there were no fear, there would be no reason to attack. Fear obscures; caution protects. Judgment is one of the most common attacks people are in the habit of using, automatically and unconsciously. Deep down, judgment masks a need for defense, or better said, a belief in that need.

Every time we judge someone else, it opens the same space in our minds for us to judge our own self-image. Among several, there are two effects produced by judgment. First, for instance, if you judge someone else's beauty or ugliness, your mind will end up reproducing the same effect in you. Why is this? Because it is the same channel. As for the same example, the second effect is that our mind becomes open to caring what other people think about us regarding appearance, and this affects how we see ourselves.

While a keen observer, through their consciousness, can skillfully observe characteristics, habits, events, and how people experience their choices, someone who judges modifies the act of observing by adding their judgments and presuppositions, which is quite different than making an assertive observation. Just observing someone's sadness means taking note of that occurrence, perhaps recognizing part of its depth and origin, but thinking or stating that someone is sad, by their very nature is a judgment. Projecting what we do not want to see in ourselves onto others is another form of judgment.

As Jesus said 2000 years ago: "Why do you look at the speck of sawdust in your brother's eye and pay no attention to the plank in your own eye?" How can you say to your brother, 'Let me take the speck out of your eye,' when all the time there is a plank in your own eye? You hypocrite, first take the plank out of your own eye, and then you will see clearly to remove the speck from your brother's eye." – New International Version – Matthew 7:3-5. Jesus' words sound like a decisive, profound invitation to self-transformation. Happy are those who make use of this wisdom.

Observation is basic. The judgment of others binds the feet of those who practice it. Labelling someone is an attempt to limit the abundance of a being. A judgment is an *established* view about someone not in keeping with who they really are. However, someone who sees light in others sees light in themselves, since it is the same light. This is also why judging someone else means judging oneself, since insofar as we express our spirit fully, we lose the need to judge. The origin of everything that we call problems lies in the idea of feeling separate from everything, of forgetting what unites us. Judging means making yourself the judge and criticizing God's signature on his work.

Before anything else, may we believe in the effect of love and respect. Thereafter, let us live accordingly. Only later, and based on that strength, may we consider the basis of other beliefs we will grow and differentiate ourselves from among so many individuals. The state of love, presence, and respect are the primary purpose, the foundation that truly transforms secondary concepts and human contexts. Therefore, if at times we feel restless about some, or other, concepts or words, let us not get caught up in long conceptual discussions. Instead, just recall the primary purpose, the true foundation behind everything. Everything else will be sorted out therein.

As we follow the path of the light of consciousness, we often face the so-called adversities; since we are elements of transformation, we move forces of light that might shake the shadows. On the other hand, those of us who are temporarily experiencing dark circumstances, lack of light, also face adversity permeated by illusions of falling back into impetuous suffering, unaware that reinvigorating spiritual support readily awaits us to work on bringing about new days. We are in peace as we live our journey in the light, because we transform adversity into opportunities, with the Love of Life always there to comfort us. Love is choosing excellence in the face of the darkness that comes up in our lives. Have you ever stopped to think about the infinite ways Love can present itself?

Love belongs to everyone, just like time. We live and flow in love in the same way we go through eternity. Nevertheless, we often vanish in a kind of presence-absence, by merely holding ourselves back in bygone periods and events to come, through the reveries of the mind's images. Likewise, as emotions come one after another, we can fade away amid feelings that overshadow love and brotherhood of the spirit. Similar to time, of which we are expanding presence, every feeling in its impermanent process directs us merely to the comfort of unconditional love.

# CHAPTER 21

P
eople hope for a book that contains the truth of Life. They
hope for a register with the laws, foundations, and meaning of
their existence. Millennia have passed, and many of us are still
searching for the *magnum opus* that will reveal the *secrets* of life. The
wholeness of Life will be available, as it already is, when human beings
*discover* that there are no secrets to Life. Everything is revealed for there
is only one of us. Truth reveals itself in our journeys just as water always
finds its way.

Nevertheless, we habitually expect the truth to be revealed by some
source other than us. If we believe that this does not include any of
us, let us reconsider revising this belief. Ask yourself if you have ever
felt the urge to read some book or another or listen to someone speak
about the truth we seek. The Bible was an attempt to meet this human
need. Although some of its content is magnificent, it does not provide
the answers to decipher reality. Let us keep in mind that, although the
recount of the main character's story is brilliantly told in the gospel,
such records came to us from third parties. Though the stories may
have contributed to the legacy, they do not convey the full magnitude of
the true events and their message. Throughout history, different books
engaged in the same effort have arisen, at times, characterizing other
religious branches.

Science emerged from this same point of view, attempting to find
truth in the workings of life, compiling it in books and then passing

it on to humanity. Many people resort to scientific works, commonly called research, convincingly saying that they have found the truth about certain subjects; however, how many people test the results of such investigations in their own lives? Many people read religious, philosophical, or other popular books like the Bible, and then affirm that now they know the truth on various subjects. However, how many have personally experienced the truth proclaimed and lived by spiritual masters and prophets?

Therefore, we uphold that there is no book containing life's truth, there is no single religion that can reconnect us with God, and there is no science that can open the doors to the absolute truth for us. We could say the same is true about the book you hold in your hands. This book cannot reveal the complete truth to you. All these sources can be wonderfully useful if properly utilized, but they only *remind us about* the truth, they are not the whole truth. Such wells of information only suggest previously lived and experienced paths, not for us to take exactly the same steps or merely proclaim words that have already been spoken. These books remind us to experience the truth in our own lives. It would be insane for us humans to widely proclaim truths we have not lived ourselves; although, if you think about it, the current state of the world is no accident.

There is only one book that contains the truth. It is not the Bible or any other religious or scientific book, not even a dictionary with the definitions of the words "truth" and "live." This book does not require us to learn new alphabets nor does its meaning get lost in translation, yet, it carries the vibrant truth. We are the living book, each one of us, all together. It is natural to every living being, and common property to us all, the very book of Life is the flow of our being and existence. We are not devaluing religion or science, quite the contrary, we praise them as living works. Nevertheless, let us remember that we have the opportunity to use no longer these means to repeat unlived truths. From this day forward, may we be the vehicles that allow the flow of truth that cannot be contained in words—the truth of what we are but of which we perceive little.

To behold Life as a mystery that reveals itself in every instant is the art of the spiritual path. To comprehend that this mystery is unendingly and constantly revealing itself is humility emerging as a foundation for individuality. Despite the existence of individuality, every man or woman is in some way connected with all human beings, as well as with each detail in the Universe. If we observe during the course of many incarnations, spirits chose to experience themselves among what was classified as red, black, white, and yellow races.

Something unprecedented is taking place in humanity's present time. Deep integration is underway. Amid globalization, the miscegenation of what has been termed as race is profoundly extending. As a result of physical interracial unions that blend different skin and hair colors, and body attributes such as size, figure, mouths, noses, and hands, not to mention customs, traditions, and knowledge. American Indians are incarnating as whites, whites as blacks, blacks as Asians, and so on, which demonstrates that we only occupy these vehicles and that there is more to us than the eye can see. Castles fall, buildings collapse, walls, homes, and bodies will tumble, but the spirit remains.

The water in your body has traveled the oceans and rains of the entire world; the minerals came from distant lands; the substances and atoms in your organism originate from stardust, energized over the course of the Universe's eternal time. Those of us here on Earth have more than just an individual body; we have a collective body as well. The Earth is part of you in such a way that our physical bodies and the Earth complement each other. The collective is within your individual body through its intense life and microscopic activity. In the same way, the Earth body also has an individual side since it operates as a great living and unified organism.

Some ancient peoples found ways to integrate with the environment, creating naturally with it instead of destroying it. These and other possibilities are available to our present civilization, including the use of technology, if well applied. Although we have many indicators that suggest otherwise—such as pollution, climate change, war and other factors, global civilization is in the process of uniting multiple civilizations—amid collective catharses and transformation—from which renewed beings are emerging to configure the nature of the new world.

That is the truth that integrates everything: we are one. Water arrives in the form of storms, descends from mountains and waterfalls, and flows through rivers and seas, just like blood flows in your veins and arteries, nourishing every nook and cranny of your body with vitality. Stones, rocks, and minerals compose the soil and terrain that form our planet, just like bones and cartilage support the foundations of your own body. Air flies to every corner, whispering as it travels long distances from where the wind comes and where it goes, as well as the breeze that gives the breath of life. Plants and vegetables, multiple species that make up the forests amid our planet's diversity and which support all forms of life, much like the organs that keep your body fully functioning. Fire emerges from within the Earth and from sunlight, presenting itself as the heat that bursts from existential forms, just as the spirit invigorates your human body with warmth and vitality.

As we remember the essence of what we have always been and always will be, soon we will see that a serpent, when it sheds its skin, shows its capacity for transformation; a bird, when it flies, flapping its wings, feels and expresses a degree of freedom; an ant, when it dedicates itself to its work, perceives the group's strength and unity; an eagle's gaze reflects its whole vision; a wolf's howling at the moon clamors for its very essence; a fish knows the depths through immersion; the running of buffaloes on the prairies is evidence of abundance and strength; a dog demonstrates its steadfast and judgment-free friendship; a cat exudes beauty and grace as it walks on the ledges; a bear finds medicinal plants to cure its own sickness. The Great Spirit is there, is here, in each of these expressions, experiencing itself in a wide variety of manifestations, integrating individual souls in the only Soul there is, the Universal Spirit—or whatever name we would like to call it.

The same way the plant feels its sap flowing within and the wind touching its edges, God feels the surging movement of the massive oceans. Just as a rock feels inclement weather, rain and erosion over time, Life feels the Earth's pulsation and tectonic movements. Like animals feel the forest, fields, or deserts, the Universe feels the celestial force of the sun and stars that dot its vastness. Just like particles feel atomic transformations and the vibrations of electrons, Light feels the stars that emit it. Similar to Humans who feel their living bodies—the dance of blood flow, the electricity of neurons and the working of their viscera and internal organs, Energy feels the body of Everything.

Earth is part of the celestial garden, just like each human existence is a leaf on the terrestrial tree. Spend a few hours contemplating the night sky, the celestial sphere, the moonlight, and the vastness of the Universe, and when you go to bed, waiting for sleep to come, see how, in fact, you are not just under the blankets, you are also falling asleep in God, amid the stars, ready to surrender.

CPSIA information can be obtained
at www.ICGtesting.com
Printed in the USA
FSHW020659040419
56958FS

9 781982 221102